# "Navigating The Chain: A Comprehensive Guide To Supply Chain Management"

by Dwayne Farr

# 1. Introduction to Supply Chain Management

Supply chain management is a multifaceted discipline that involves the coordination and integration of all activities involved in the sourcing, procurement, production, and logistics processes that deliver products or services to customers. It encompasses the seamless flow of goods, information, and finances across various stages, from raw material extraction to the end consumer.

In today's globalized and interconnected world, supply chain management is becoming increasingly crucial for organizations to gain a competitive advantage. Effective supply chain management goes beyond streamlining operations; it requires a strategic approach that optimizes processes and relationships between suppliers, manufacturers, distributors, retailers, and customers.

The primary goal of supply chain management is to maximize customer value while minimizing costs and risks. By improving efficiency and responsiveness, organizations can meet customer demands effectively, reduce lead times, manage inventory levels, and enhance overall customer satisfaction. The effective management of the supply chain contributes to improved operational performance, increased profitability, and enhanced competitiveness in the market.

The concept of supply chain management has evolved significantly over the years. Initially, it primarily focused on logistical operations within a firm, with the primary objective of efficiently moving goods from one point to another. However, with the advent of technology and the rise of globalization, the scope of supply chain management expanded to include wider strategic planning, collaboration, and coordination among various stakeholders.

Nowadays, organizations recognize the strategic value of supply chain management and its impact on business success. It is not merely a cost center but a critical driver of value creation and customer satisfaction. Supply chain professionals play a pivotal role in enhancing supply chain efficiency, flexibility, and responsiveness while ensuring sustainable practices and ethical considerations are taken into account.

Supply chain management encompasses a range of activities, each with its own set of challenges and opportunities. Some of the key components of supply chain management include:

1. Strategic Planning: Strategic planning involves aligning supply chain goals with the overall business strategy, identifying key performance indicators, and developing strategies to achieve competitive advantage and meet customer demands. It requires a thorough understanding of market dynamics, customer preferences, and organizational capabilities.

2. Supplier Relationship Management: Supplier relationship management focuses on developing collaborative partnerships with suppliers, fostering long-term relationships, managing contracts, and ensuring a reliable and efficient supply base. Effective supplier relationships enable organizations to optimize costs, enhance quality, reduce lead times, and drive innovation.

3. Inventory Optimization: Inventory optimization aims to strike a balance between adequate stock levels to meet customer demands and minimizing excess inventory costs. By implementing robust inventory management practices, organizations can optimize the use of working capital, minimize stockouts, and improve overall supply chain agility.

4. Distribution and Logistics: Distribution and logistics involve managing transportation, warehousing, order fulfillment, and reverse logistics to ensure goods are delivered to the right place at the right time. Efficient logistics operations contribute to reduced lead times, lower transportation costs, improved customer service, and effective product flow.

5. Technology Integration: Technology integration plays a vital role in supply chain management, enabling efficient data collection, real-time visibility, automation, and analytics. Technologies such as Enterprise Resource Planning (ERP) systems, Warehouse Management Systems (WMS), Transportation Management Systems (TMS), and Supply Chain Analytics provide valuable insights and enable informed decision-making.

6. Sustainability: Sustainability is an increasingly important aspect of supply chain management, as organizations strive to reduce their environmental impact, promote social responsibility, and adopt sustainable practices throughout the supply chain. This includes minimizing waste, optimizing packaging, reducing carbon emissions, and ensuring ethical sourcing practices.

7. Risk Management: Risk management is a critical component of supply chain management, as it helps organizations identify, assess, and mitigate risks that could disrupt the supply chain. This includes risks associated with demand volatility, natural disasters, geopolitical factors, supplier failures, and cyber threats. Developing robust risk management strategies and contingency plans is essential to ensure business continuity and minimize disruptions.

8. Demand Forecasting: Demand forecasting is another key aspect of supply chain management. Accurate demand forecasting helps organizations optimize inventory levels, improve production planning, and meet customer expectations. By analyzing historical data, market trends, and customer insights, organizations can make informed decisions regarding production, procurement, and distribution.

9. Lean Principles: Lean principles, derived from the Toyota Production System, aim to eliminate waste and improve overall efficiency in the supply chain. Techniques such as Just-In-Time (JIT) production, value stream mapping, and continuous improvement help streamline processes, reduce lead times, and enhance overall productivity.

10. Performance Metrics: Performance metrics form the foundation of measuring and evaluating supply chain performance. Key performance indicators (KPIs) such as on-time delivery, order accuracy, inventory turnover, forecast accuracy, and customer satisfaction enable organizations to track progress, identify areas for improvement, and make data-driven decisions.

Looking into the future, supply chain management is anticipated to undergo further transformation. Factors such as technological advancements, the rise of e-commerce, changing consumer behaviors, and globalization will continue to shape the supply chain landscape. Organizations will need to embrace digitization, emerging technologies (e.g., blockchain, Internet of Things), foster collaboration, and continuously adapt to meet evolving customer expectations efficiently.

This book explores the principles, strategies, and best practices in supply chain management, providing real-world case studies and practical insights. Whether you are a business professional, student, or enthusiast, the knowledge and tools gained from this book will equip you to navigate the complexities of supply chain management successfully.

Now, let us embark on this journey through the fascinating world of supply chain management and uncover the secrets to achieving operational excellence and driving business growth.

---

# 2. Historical Evolution of Supply Chains

Supply chains have been an essential part of human civilization for thousands of years. From the earliest days of trade and barter to the complex global networks we see today, supply chains have played a fundamental role in connecting producers and consumers.

The roots of supply chains can be traced back to ancient civilizations such as the Mesopotamians, Egyptians, and Romans. These societies relied on trade routes to exchange goods and resources over long distances. They established networks of caravans, river transportation, and even seafaring vessels to facilitate the movement of goods. Along these trade routes, various intermediaries emerged to ensure the safe arrival and distribution of goods. These intermediaries, known as middlemen, played a crucial role in bridging the gap between producers and consumers, facilitating transactions, and managing storage and transportation.

The development of supply chains took significant strides during the Industrial Revolution in the 18th and 19th centuries. This period brought about groundbreaking advancements in transportation, communication, and manufacturing processes. The invention of the steam engine revolutionized transportation, allowing goods to be moved faster and in greater quantities than ever before. It also paved the way for the establishment of rail and canal networks, effectively connecting different regions and enabling the efficient movement of goods.

Simultaneously, advancements in manufacturing techniques led to increased production rates. Henry Ford's introduction of the assembly line production system in the early 20th century revolutionized manufacturing processes once again. The assembly line enabled the division of labor, where each worker specialized in a specific task, creating a more streamlined and efficient production process. This innovation marked the beginning of mass production, significantly reducing costs and making goods more affordable for consumers worldwide.

The mid-20th century witnessed further advancements in supply chain management with the introduction of computer technology. The use of computers enabled better inventory control, demand forecasting, and logistics optimization. Companies could now track inventory levels in real-time, identify demand patterns, and adjust production and distribution accordingly. This marked the advent of just-in-time (JIT) manufacturing, a concept popularized by companies like Toyota, where materials and parts are delivered precisely when needed, reducing waste and improving overall efficiency.

Globalization in the late 20th and early 21st centuries brought about a new wave of transformation for supply chains. Companies began to source raw materials, components, and labor from different countries to capitalize on cost advantages and access larger markets. This led to the establishment of multinational supply chains, involving complex networks of suppliers, manufacturers, distributors, and retailers spread across different continents. These supply chains required sophisticated coordination, communication, and transportation systems to ensure the smooth flow of goods across borders.

However, the historical evolution of supply chains has not been without challenges and disruptions. Natural disasters, political instability, economic downturns, and the recent COVID-19 pandemic have highlighted the vulnerabilities inherent in global supply chains. Companies have had to adapt to these disruptions by implementing proactive risk management strategies and developing robust contingency plans.

In recent years, supply chain management has also faced increasing scrutiny regarding sustainability and ethical practices. Consumers and stakeholders are demanding greater transparency and accountability throughout the supply chain. There is a growing emphasis on responsible sourcing, fair labor practices, environmental conservation, and reducing carbon footprints. Companies are now integrating sustainability principles and traceability solutions to ensure that their supply chains are socially and environmentally responsible.

The historical evolution of supply chains has been driven by numerous factors, including technological advancements, economic transformations, and changing consumer demands. From ancient trade routes to modern-day global networks, supply chains have continuously adapted to meet the evolving needs of societies.

The journey of supply chain management is far from over, as ongoing innovation and the integration of emerging technologies promise to shape the future of supply chains in ways we can only imagine.

One of the emerging technologies that is expected to have a significant impact on supply chains is the Internet of Things (IoT). IoT refers to the network of interconnected devices, sensors, and machines that can communicate and share data with each other. In the context of supply chains, IoT can provide real-time visibility and tracking of goods throughout the entire supply chain, enabling companies to monitor and manage inventory levels, detect and resolve bottlenecks, and improve overall efficiency.

Another technology that holds great potential for supply chain management is blockchain.

Blockchain is a decentralized and transparent digital ledger that allows for secure and immutable recording of transactions. This technology can enhance supply chain visibility and traceability by creating a permanent and tamper-proof record of every transaction and movement of goods. Blockchain can also facilitate the implementation of smart contracts that automatically execute contractual obligations once predefined conditions are met. This can simplify and streamline complex supply chain processes, such as payments, customs clearance, and quality control.

Artificial Intelligence (AI) and machine learning are also expected to play a significant role in transforming supply chains. AI-powered algorithms can analyze vast amounts of data and provide valuable insights for demand forecasting, inventory optimization, and route planning. Machine learning models can constantly learn and adapt to changing market conditions, enabling more accurate predictions and intelligent decision-making.

Furthermore, robotics and automation technologies are revolutionizing warehouse and distribution operations. Robots can handle repetitive and physically demanding tasks, leading to increased efficiency and reduced human error. Autonomous vehicles, such as drones and self-driving trucks, can streamline transportation operations, reduce delivery times, and lower overall costs.

Additionally, supply chains are now embracing the concept of circular economy, which focuses on reducing waste, reusing materials, and recycling resources. Instead of the traditional linear model of "take-make-use-dispose," companies are redesigning products and packaging to maximize their lifespan and minimize environmental impact. By implementing circular supply chain practices, companies can create a more sustainable and resilient system that considers the entire lifecycle of products.

The historical evolution of supply chains has been a continuous journey of innovation, adaptation, and resilience. As we move forward, supply chain professionals and companies need to embrace emerging technologies, sustainability principles, and risk management strategies to thrive in an ever-changing global landscape. The future of supply chains holds great promise, and it is up to us to shape it in a way that benefits not only businesses but also society and the planet as a whole.

---

# 3. Key Components of a Supply Chain

A supply chain is a complex network of organizations, activities, information, and resources involved in the production, distribution, and delivery of goods and services to customers. Understanding the key components that make up a supply chain is crucial for effective management and optimization.

1. Suppliers: The first component of a supply chain is the suppliers who provide raw materials, components, or services to the organization. Selecting and managing these suppliers is essential to ensure a consistent and reliable supply of inputs. Organizations need to consider factors like supplier capabilities, reliability, quality, price, and ethical practices while choosing their supplier base. Maintaining strong supplier relationships through regular communication, performance evaluation, and collaboration helps in ensuring timely delivery and quality standards.

2. Procurement: Procurement refers to the process of purchasing goods or services from suppliers. It involves activities such as sourcing, negotiation, ordering, and payment. Effective procurement practices can lead to cost savings, quality improvement, and better supplier relationships. Strategic sourcing involves analyzing market trends, identifying potential suppliers, and negotiating favorable contracts. Organizations can also implement e-procurement systems to automate and streamline procurement processes, reducing paperwork and errors while increasing efficiency.

3. Production: The production component of a supply chain involves the transformation of raw materials into finished products or services. This can happen through various processes such as manufacturing, assembly, or value-added services. Efficient production processes are essential to meet customer demand and optimize resources.

Techniques like lean manufacturing and just-in-time (JIT) production are commonly used to eliminate waste, reduce lead times, and improve operational efficiency. Lean manufacturing focuses on identifying and eliminating non-value-added activities, while JIT production aims to produce goods only when they are needed, reducing inventory holding costs and potential waste. Organizations can also implement advanced technologies like robotics, automation, and machine learning to enhance productivity and quality control.

4. Inventory Management: Inventory management involves controlling and monitoring the stock of raw materials, work-in-progress, and finished goods. This component ensures that the right amount of inventory is available at the right time to meet customer demand while minimizing storage costs and obsolescence. Effective inventory management strategies involve optimizing inventory levels, implementing inventory forecasting techniques, improving order fulfillment processes, and employing inventory optimization tools and software.

Techniques such as ABC analysis, economic order quantity, and safety stock management help in maintaining appropriate inventory levels based on the criticality of items. ABC analysis categorizes items into A, B, or C classes based on their value or frequency of use. Economic order quantity helps determine the optimal order quantity considering cost factors, while safety stock management ensures a buffer against unexpected demand fluctuations.

5. Warehousing and Distribution: Warehousing and distribution involve the storage and movement of goods within the supply chain network. Warehouses act as intermediaries between production and distribution, providing a central location for inventory management and order fulfillment. Distribution activities focus on delivering products to customers through various channels such as retailers, wholesalers, or direct-to-consumer.

Efficient warehouse management includes optimizing warehouse layout, implementing inventory tracking systems, employing efficient picking and packing processes, and utilizing technologies like Radio Frequency Identification (RFID) for real-time tracking and visibility of inventory. Warehouse layout optimization considers factors like stock density, product flow, labor efficiency, and safety. Inventory tracking systems help monitor inventory levels, track item location, and enable efficient order picking and replenishment processes. RFID technology enables automated identification, data capture, and real-time visibility of goods, enhancing supply chain efficiency.

6. Transportation: Transportation is a critical component that connects different stages of the supply chain by moving goods from one location to another. It includes selecting appropriate modes of transportation, managing logistics providers, optimizing routes, and tracking shipments.

Efficient transportation helps in reducing lead times, improving customer satisfaction, and minimizing costs. Organizations can consider factors like transportation costs, transit time, reliability, sustainability, and infrastructure capabilities while selecting transportation modes. Road, rail, air, sea, or intermodal transportation options can be evaluated based on the specific requirements of the supply chain. Advanced transportation management systems (TMS), route optimization software, and real-time tracking systems enable organizations to enhance visibility, streamline logistics operations, and optimize transportation costs.

7. Information Systems and Technology: Information systems and technology play a vital role in managing and coordinating supply chain activities. This component includes technologies such as Enterprise Resource Planning (ERP), Supply Chain Management (SCM) software, electronic data interchange (EDI), and real-time tracking systems. These systems facilitate accurate and timely information sharing, collaborative planning, and data-driven decision-making.

Organizations can integrate their internal systems with those of their suppliers, customers, and logistics partners to improve visibility, collaboration, and overall supply chain performance. Technologies such as the Internet of Things (IoT), Big Data analytics, and Artificial Intelligence (AI) can further enhance supply chain capabilities by providing actionable insights, predictive analytics, and automation. IoT enables real-time monitoring of assets, inventory, and environmental conditions, while Big Data analytics helps transform data into meaningful insights for decision-making. AI-based technologies assist in demand forecasting, route optimization, inventory optimization, and predictive maintenance, among other applications.

8. Demand Management: Demand management involves understanding and forecasting customer demand to align supply chain activities accordingly. It includes activities such as demand planning, forecasting, order management, and customer relationship management.

Effective demand management ensures that the right products are available in the right quantities and locations to meet customer expectations. Organizations can adopt different demand forecasting techniques like statistical models, market research, and collaborative planning with key customers to minimize forecast errors. Demand-driven replenishment strategies like Vendor Managed Inventory (VMI) or Continuous Replenishment Programs (CRP) can help organizations respond promptly to changes in customer demand.

Demand planning software and advanced analytics tools can assist in demand segmentation, forecasting accuracy, and scenario planning. By analyzing historical data, market trends, and customer behavior, organizations can improve forecast accuracy and optimize inventory levels. Collaborative planning with customers and suppliers can help in aligning plans, sharing information, and improving overall supply chain responsiveness.

9. Customer Service: Customer service is a crucial component that ensures customer satisfaction throughout the supply chain process. It includes activities such as order processing, order tracking, after-sales service, and handling customer inquiries or complaints.

Providing excellent customer service enhances brand reputation, customer loyalty, and repeat business. Organizations can invest in customer relationship management (CRM) systems to effectively manage customer interactions and address their needs. Employing customer-centric strategies like personalized experiences, proactive communication, and quick issue resolution contributes to customer satisfaction and retention.

Customer service centers, online portals, and self-service options can enable customers to place orders, track shipments, and access information conveniently. Timely and accurate order fulfillment, proactive communication, efficient complaint handling, and easy returns and exchanges are key aspects of effective customer service. Organizations can use customer feedback, surveys, and performance metrics like Net Promoter Score (NPS) to measure and improve customer satisfaction and loyalty.

10. Performance Measurement: Performance measurement involves tracking and evaluating supply chain performance using key performance indicators (KPIs). These KPIs can include metrics such as on-time delivery, inventory turnover, customer satisfaction, cost-to-serve, and supplier performance.

Measuring performance helps identify areas for improvement, benchmark against industry standards, and ensure alignment with strategic objectives. Organizations can leverage advanced analytics tools and dashboards to visualize and analyze supply chaindata in real-time. This allows for timely decision-making and proactive problem-solving.

Commonly used supply chain performance metrics include:

- On-time delivery: Measures the percentage of orders delivered to customers on or before the promised date. It reflects supply chain reliability and customer service levels.

- Order fulfillment cycle time: Measures the time taken to process and fulfill customer orders, from order receipt to delivery. A shorter cycle time indicates improved efficiency and responsiveness.

- Inventory turnover: Measures the number of times inventory is sold and replaced within a specific period. It reflects how effectively inventory is managed and controlled.

- Perfect order rate: Measures the percentage of orders that are delivered to customers without any errors or defects. It assesses supply chain accuracy and order fulfillment capabilities.

- Supply chain costs: Measures the total costs incurred to operate the supply chain, including procurement, production, transportation, and warehousing costs. It helps evaluate cost-efficiency and identify areas for cost reduction.

- Supplier performance: Measures the performance of suppliers in terms of delivery reliability, quality, responsiveness, and adherence to contractual terms. It helps in supplier evaluation, selection, and relationship management.

- Customer satisfaction: Measures the level of customer satisfaction with the products, services, and overall experience provided by the supply chain. It can be assessed through surveys, feedback, and ratings.

- Sustainability metrics: Measures the environmental and social impact of the supply chain, such as carbon emissions, energy consumption, waste generation, and labor practices. It helps in assessing sustainability performance and identifying areas for improvement.

By regularly monitoring and analyzing these performance metrics, organizations can gain insights into their supply chain performance, identify areas for improvement, and make data-driven decisions. Continuous improvement initiatives, such as Lean Six Sigma and Kaizen, can be employed to drive operational excellence and enhance supply chain performance.

In conclusion, understanding the key components of a supply chain is crucial for effective management and optimization. From suppliers to customers, each component plays a vital role in ensuring the smooth flow of goods and services. By focusing on areas such as procurement, production, inventory management, warehousing, transportation, information systems and technology, demand management, customer service, and performance measurement, organizations can improve supply chain efficiency, reduce costs, enhance customer satisfaction, and achieve a competitive advantage in the market.

---

# 4. Strategic Planning in Supply Chain Management

Strategic planning is a vital component of effective supply chain management. It involves aligning the supply chain strategy with the overall business strategy to ensure a cohesive and integrated approach. This chapter explores the key aspects of strategic planning in supply chain management and provides deep insights into its importance in driving organizational success.

1. Understanding the Business Strategy:

In order to develop a robust supply chain strategy, it is crucial to start by gaining a deep understanding of the overall business strategy. This includes identifying the company's mission, vision, and objectives. By understanding the business strategy, supply chain professionals can ensure that their strategies are fully aligned with and supportive of the broader organizational goals.

Furthermore, it is essential to analyze the competitive landscape and market demands. By understanding key market trends, customer preferences, and competitors' strategies, organizations can develop a supply chain strategy that is agile and responsive to market dynamics.

2. Setting Supply Chain Objectives:

Once the business strategy is clear, it is imperative to set specific supply chain objectives that align with the overall business goals. These objectives should be SMART (Specific, Measurable, Achievable, Relevant, Time-bound) to provide a clear focus and direction for supply chain activities.

Supply chain objectives typically encompass areas such as customer service levels, cost reduction, quality improvement, sustainability, and innovation. For example, objectives may include reducing lead times, improving order accuracy, optimizing inventory levels, enhancing supply chain visibility, or developing sustainable sourcing practices.

3. Assessing the Current Supply Chain:

To develop an effective supply chain strategy, a comprehensive assessment of the current supply chain should be conducted. This assessment includes analyzing various aspects such as the existing network design, sourcing and procurement practices, distribution channels, inventory management, and technology infrastructure.

By evaluating the current state of the supply chain, organizations can identify inefficiencies, bottlenecks, and areas of improvement. This analysis helps in identifying strengths and weaknesses and provides a foundation for developing a targeted strategic plan.

4. Gap Analysis and Scenario Planning:

Based on the assessment, a gap analysis should be conducted to identify the gaps between the current state and the desired future state of the supply chain. This analysis helps in understanding the challenges and opportunities that need to be addressed in the strategic planning process.

In addition to the gap analysis, scenario planning can be employed to analyze different possible futures and develop strategies that can adapt to various market conditions and uncertainties. This allows organizations to develop flexible supply chain strategies that can withstand change and disruptions.

5. Designing the Supply Chain Strategy:

Once the relevant information is gathered, the supply chain strategy should be designed to align with the identified objectives, address the identified gaps, and capitalize on the strategic opportunities.

The design of the supply chain strategy includes determining the optimal network configuration, selecting the appropriate sourcing and procurement strategies, designing efficient distribution and logistics channels, and integrating advanced technologies and systems. It also involves considering risk management, sustainability, and collaboration with key stakeholders.

Network design involves evaluating the number and location of facilities, such as manufacturing plants, warehouses, and distribution centers, to achieve a balance between costs, responsiveness, and customer service. It includes considerations of factors like proximity to suppliers, customers, and transportation infrastructure.

Sourcing and procurement strategies involve evaluating the make-or-buy decisions, selecting suppliers, and establishing strategic partnerships. Organizations need to assess supplier capabilities, pricing, quality, reliability, and ethical practices. The selection process should consider the overall value proposition and the alignment with sustainability and corporate social responsibility goals.

Efficient distribution and logistics channels focus on optimizing transportation modes, warehouse operations, order fulfillment processes, and information flow. This involves selecting the most effective transportation modes, optimizing routing, and leveraging technology solutions such as warehouse management systems and transportation management systems.

Furthermore, supply chain strategy should incorporate a clear plan for talent development and human resource management. Recognizing that people are critical to executing the strategy, organizations must invest in training, recruitment, and retention efforts to build a capable and skilled supply chain workforce.

6. Implementation and Execution:

Once the supply chain strategy is developed, successful implementation and execution become paramount. This involves effectively communicating the strategy to the relevant stakeholders, allocating resources, establishing performance metrics, and monitoring progress.

Organizations need to create a culture of accountability and ensure that the necessary tools and technology are in place to support the execution of the strategy. Additionally, regular reviews and adjustments should be made to ensure the strategic plans remain relevant and effective in a dynamic business environment.

7. Continuous Improvement and Evaluation:

Strategic planning is an ongoing process, and continuous improvement and evaluation are necessary to ensure the supply chain strategy remains aligned with evolving business needs.

This includes analyzing performance metrics, conducting regular benchmarking, seeking feedback from customers and suppliers, and identifying areas for optimization. Organizations need to embrace a culture of continuous improvement and leverage emerging technologies, such as artificial intelligence and data analytics, to drive innovation and make informed decisions.

Supply chain risk management is a critical aspect of continuous improvement. Organizations need to proactively identify and mitigate potential risks, such as disruptions in suppliers, transportation disruptions, political instability, or natural disasters. This may involve developing contingency plans, diversifying suppliers, and implementing robust monitoring systems.

By proactively adapting to changes, organizations can position themselves for long-term success and maintain a competitive edge in an increasingly complex and interconnected global marketplace.

In conclusion, strategic planning plays a critical role in supply chain management by aligning the supply chain strategy with the overall business strategy. It provides a roadmap for achieving organizational goals, improving efficiency, enhancing customer satisfaction, and gaining a competitive advantage. By carefully designing and implementing effective supply chain strategies, organizations can position themselves for long-term success in an ever-evolving business landscape.

———————

# 5. Supplier Relationship Management

In today's interconnected business world, successful supply chain management heavily relies on the strength of relationships with suppliers. Supplier Relationship Management (SRM) is a vital component of any effective supply chain strategy. It involves fostering and leveraging relationships with suppliers to drive mutual value, optimize costs, and ensure the consistent delivery of high-quality goods and services.

The goal of SRM is to develop long-term, strategic partnerships with key suppliers. These partnerships go beyond short-term transactional relationships and foster collaboration, trust, and mutual growth opportunities. By working closely with suppliers, organizations can enhance supply chain efficiency, reduce operational risks, and gain a competitive edge in the market.

To effectively manage supplier relationships, organizations need to adopt certain key practices and principles. These include:

1. Supplier Selection: Careful evaluation and selection of suppliers is crucial. Organizations should assess suppliers based on their capabilities, track record, financial stability, and alignment with strategic goals. Evaluating suppliers based on their ethical and sustainable practices is also becoming increasingly important in today's socially conscious marketplace. Supplier evaluation should consider factors such as diversity, social responsibility, environmental impact, and adherence to ethical business practices.

2. Contract Management: Establishing clear contracts and agreements with suppliers is essential to ensure mutual understanding, define expectations, and minimize potential conflicts or misunderstandings. Well-drafted contracts should include provisions for quality control, delivery schedules, pricing, intellectual property rights, and dispute resolution mechanisms. Additionally, organizations should emphasize long-term contracts to provide stability and foster stronger relationships with suppliers.

3. Communication and Collaboration: Open and transparent communication is vital for building strong relationships with suppliers. Regular meetings, joint planning sessions, and effective information sharing can foster collaboration and enable proactive problem-solving. Communication should not be limited to day-to-day operations but should include

strategic discussions to align goals and explore opportunities for innovation. Sharing forecasts, market trends, and customer insights can enable suppliers to better understand the organization's needs and adjust their processes accordingly.

4. Performance Evaluation: Monitoring and assessing supplier performance is critical to drive continuous improvement. Key performance indicators (KPIs) should be established to track metrics such as quality, delivery, responsiveness, and overall value provided by the supplier. Regular performance reviews should be conducted, and feedback should be shared to ensure both parties are aligned in their efforts. Incorporating supplier scorecards and performance-based incentives can further motivate suppliers to consistently meet or exceed expectations.

5. Supplier Development: Organizations should actively support and contribute to the development of their suppliers. This can involve providing training, sharing best practices, and assisting in process improvements to enhance supplier capabilities. Collaboration in product development and innovation can further strengthen the relationship and create mutual competitive advantage. Organizations can also foster supplier diversity by working with small and diverse suppliers, thereby promoting inclusive business practices and expanding their supplier base.

6. Risk Management: Identifying and mitigating risks associated with suppliers is crucial to avoid disruptions in the supply chain. Regular risk assessments and contingency plans should be in place to address potential vulnerabilities. Organizations should also explore alternative sources of supply and maintain good relationships with secondary suppliers to have backup options in case of emergencies or unforeseen circumstances. Collaborative risk management activities, such as joint audits, can help identify and address potential risks together.

7. Relationship Governance: Establishing clear governance structures and processes ensures effective management of supplier relationships. Roles and responsibilities should be defined, and regular reviews and performance discussions should take place to address any challenges or opportunities. A dedicated supplier relationship management team can be responsible for overseeing the overall strategy, monitoring supplier performance, and driving continuous improvement in supplier relationships. Involving cross-functional teams from different departments, such as procurement, operations, quality assurance, and finance, can provide a holistic perspective and strengthen the effectiveness of relationship governance.

By adopting these practices, organizations can create a robust Supplier Relationship Management framework that enhances collaboration, drives innovation, and maximizes value from their supplier partnerships. Effective SRM enables organizations to streamline processes, reduce costs, improve product quality, and ultimately meet the needs and expectations of their customers in a competitive marketplace.

In today's dynamic business environment, where supply chains are becoming increasingly global and complex, it is essential for organizations to prioritize Supplier Relationship Management as a key strategic initiative. Building strong and collaborative relationships with suppliers not only ensures a reliable supply of goods and services but also contributes to the overall success and sustainability of the organization. By investing in long-term partnerships, organizations can gain a competitive advantage, foster innovation, and create a resilient supply chain that can adapt to changing market conditions. Furthermore, embracing technological advancements such as supplier management software, data analytics, and artificial intelligence can enhance the efficiency and effectiveness of SRM, allowing organizations to leverage data-driven insights to further optimize their supplier relationships. Constantly evolving and improving SRM practices will enable organizations to forge stronger, more resilient supplier partnerships that drive long-term success in today's rapidly changing business landscape.

---

# 6. Inventory Optimization and Management

Inventory management is a critical aspect of supply chain management as it directly impacts a company's profitability and customer satisfaction. Effective inventory management ensures that the right products are available in the right quantities, at the right locations, and at the right time.

6.1 Importance of Inventory Optimization

Inventory optimization is the process of determining the right levels of inventory to meet demand while minimizing costs. It aims to strike a balance between having enough stock to fulfill orders and avoiding excess inventory that ties up capital and increases holding costs.

An optimized inventory brings several benefits to a business:
1. Reduced Stockouts: Maintaining optimal inventory levels helps avoid stockouts, ensuring that products are available to fulfill customer orders promptly. This enhances customer satisfaction and prevents lost sales opportunities.
2. Minimized Holding Costs: Excessive inventory ties up capital, incurs warehousing costs, and increases the risk of obsolescence or spoilage. By optimizing inventory levels, businesses can optimize cash flow, reduce storage costs, and minimize losses due to inventory write-offs.
3. Increased Efficiency: Well-managed inventory leads to improved operational efficiency. When the right products are available at the right time, it eliminates delays and improves the flow of goods throughout the supply chain. This results in shorter lead times, reduced production downtime, and improved order fulfillment speeds.
4. Improved Supply Chain Visibility: Effective inventory management enhances supply chain visibility by providing real-time data on stock levels, movement, and demand patterns. This visibility allows businesses to identify bottlenecks, mitigate risks, and make informed decisions on procurement, production, and distribution.
5. Cost Savings: Inventory optimization reduces both holding costs and stockout costs, resulting in overall cost savings for the business. It allows companies to maintain optimal inventory levels, avoiding unnecessary expenses associated with excess inventory while ensuring availability to meet customer demand.

6.2 Inventory Management Strategies

To optimize inventory levels effectively, companies can employ various inventory management strategies tailored to their specific needs:

### 6.2.1 Just-in-Time (JIT)

The just-in-time (JIT) strategy focuses on minimizing or eliminating inventory by receiving materials or products just in time for production or customer delivery. It relies on tight coordination between suppliers and the company. JIT reduces holding costs, eliminates waste, and improves responsiveness to customer demand.

To implement JIT effectively, companies engage in close collaboration with suppliers to ensure reliable and timely deliveries. Accurate demand forecasting becomes crucial to synchronize production schedules and align with customer requirements. JIT may require investments in technology, such as Electronic Data Interchange (EDI) systems, to facilitate seamless communication and automate ordering processes between suppliers and the company.

### 6.2.2 Economic Order Quantity (EOQ)

EOQ is a classic inventory management model that determines the optimal order quantity to minimize total inventory costs. It takes into account variables such as ordering costs, carrying costs, and demand patterns. EOQ helps companies strike a balance between stockout costs and holding costs.

To calculate EOQ, businesses analyze historical demand data, supplier lead times, and costs associated with ordering and carrying inventory. This model helps in identifying the order quantity that minimizes the total cost while ensuring sufficient stock availability. However, it requires regular monitoring and adjustment as demand patterns, costs, and lead times may fluctuate over time.

### 6.2.3 ABC Analysis

ABC analysis categorizes inventory items based on their value and contribution to sales. Class A items are high-value products with high sales volume, while Class C items are low-value products with low sales volume. This analysis helps prioritize inventory management efforts, focusing on the most critical items.

By classifying inventory items, businesses can allocate resources and attention to the most important products. Class A items may require more frequent monitoring, tighter control, and closer collaboration with suppliers to avoid stockouts. Class C items, on the other hand, may undergo less frequent review, allowing more resources to be allocated to higher-value items. ABC analysis facilitates effective inventory planning and improves resource allocation.

## 6.3 Inventory Optimization Techniques

While inventory management strategies provide a framework, implementing various inventory optimization techniques helps companies achieve optimal inventory levels:

### 6.3.1 Demand Forecasting

Accurate demand forecasting is vital for inventory optimization. Businesses analyze historical sales data, market trends, and statistical models to forecast future demand with accuracy. By forecasting demand, companies can adjust inventory levels accordingly, ensuring adequate stock availability while avoiding excess inventory.

To improve the accuracy of demand forecasting, businesses can leverage advanced technologies such as machine learning algorithms or demand sensing tools. These technologies enable the analysis of large datasets, real-time data integration, and predictive modeling, resulting in more precise demand forecasts.

### 6.3.2 Safety Stock

Safety stock acts as a buffer to mitigate uncertainties in demand and supply. It protects against unexpected fluctuations, delays, or disruptions in the supply chain. Determining the appropriate safety stock level involves considering factors such as lead times, demand variability, and desired service levels.

To calculate safety stock, businesses assess historical demand variability, supplier lead time variability, and desired service levels. By maintaining an appropriate safety stock, companies can handle unexpected demand spikes or supply disruptions without experiencing stockouts. Safety stock should be regularly reviewed and adjusted based on changing business conditions and market dynamics.

### 6.3.3 Inventory Centralization and Visibility

Centralizing inventory across multiple locations can improve visibility and control. By having a centralized view of inventory levels and movement, companies can optimize stock levels, avoid duplication, and streamline inventory management processes. Advanced technology and systems enable real-time tracking and coordination.

Inventory centralization allows businesses to consolidate stock, reducing excess inventory across multiple locations. It enhances visibility into stock levels and movement, enabling accurate demand forecasting and order fulfillment planning. Centralized inventory data also facilitates better coordination with suppliers, enabling more efficient replenishment processes.

### 6.3.4 Vendor-Managed Inventory (VMI)

Vendor-Managed Inventory (VMI) is a strategy where suppliers monitor and replenish their customers' inventory levels. Suppliers take responsibility for maintaining appropriate stock levels based on data shared by customers. VMI improves supply chain visibility, reduces the risk of stockouts, and minimizes holding costs for both parties.

To implement VMI, companies collaborate closely with suppliers and establish data-sharing agreements. Suppliers proactively monitor inventory levels, track demand patterns, and initiate replenishment based on agreed-upon triggers. This approach reduces the administrative burden on customers, strengthens supplier-customer relationships, and ensures optimal stock availability.

### 6.4 Evaluation and Performance Measurement

Effective inventory management requires ongoing evaluation and performance measurement. Key performance indicators (KPIs) play a crucial role in assessing inventory performance. Some commonly used KPIs include:

1. Inventory Turnover Ratio: This ratio measures the number of times inventory is sold or used during a specified period. A high turnover ratio indicates efficient inventory management, while a low ratio may indicate excess inventory.

2. Fill Rate: Fill rate measures the percentage of customer orders that are completely fulfilled from available stock. A high fill rate indicates that the business is meeting customer demand promptly, while a low fill rate may indicate stockouts or insufficient inventory.

3. Stockout Rate: Stockout rate measures the percentage of customer orders that cannot be fulfilled due to stockouts. It reflects the availability and accuracy of inventory levels. A low stockout rate indicates effective inventory management and customer service.

4. Order Cycle Time: Order cycle time measures the time taken from order placement to order fulfillment. A shorter order cycle time indicates efficient inventory management and faster order fulfillment.

5. Holding Cost: Holding cost indicates the cost of holding inventory over a specified period. It includes costs such as storage, insurance, obsolescence, and capital tied up in inventory. A lower holding cost indicates better inventory management and cost optimization.

6. Order Accuracy: Order accuracy measures the percentage of orders that are fulfilled correctly without errors or discrepancies. A high order accuracy rate indicates effective inventory management and order fulfillment processes.

By regularly monitoring and analyzing these KPIs, companies can identify areas for improvement, track progress towards inventory optimization goals, and make informed decisions on inventory management strategies.

6.5 Challenges and Considerations

Implementing inventory optimization and management strategies comes with certain challenges and considerations:

1. Data Accuracy and Integration: Accurate inventory data is crucial for effective inventory management. Data discrepancies or errors can lead to inaccurate forecasts, stockouts, or overstocking. Ensuring data integrity and integration across systems is essential for accurate demand forecasting and inventory planning.

2. Demand Volatility: Fluctuating customer demand can make inventory management challenging. Unpredictable demand patterns can lead to stockouts or excess inventory. Businesses must invest in robust demand forecasting methods and agile inventory management systems to adapt to changing demand patterns.

3. Seasonality and Promotions: Seasonal demand variations and promotional activities can strain inventory management. Businesses must anticipate and plan for these fluctuations to maintain optimal stock levels while avoiding stockouts or excess inventory during peak periods.

4. Supply Chain Collaboration: Effective inventory management requires close collaboration with suppliers and partners. Businesses must establish strong relationships, implement effective communication channels, and share data to ensure timely and accurate replenishments and minimize lead times.

5. Technology and Automation: Leveraging technology and automation can enhance inventory management efficiency. Implementing advanced inventory management systems, demand forecasting tools, and real-time tracking solutions can improve visibility, streamline processes, and optimize inventory levels.

6.6 Conclusion

Inventory optimization and management are critical components of supply chain management. By implementing effective strategies and techniques, businesses can achieve optimal inventory levels, minimize costs, and enhance customer satisfaction. Accurate demand forecasting, safety stock management, centralization of inventory, and collaboration with suppliers are key factors in successful inventory optimization. Ongoing evaluation and performance measurement through KPIs help track progress and identify areas for improvement. Despite challenges such as data accuracy, demand volatility, and supply chain collaboration, businesses can overcome these obstacles by leveraging technology, automation, and best practices in inventory management.

---

# 7. Distribution and Logistics Strategies

In the modern business landscape, distribution and logistics strategies play a crucial role in ensuring the smooth flow of products from manufacturers to end consumers. These strategies involve the planning, coordination, and execution of various activities such as transportation, warehousing, inventory management, order fulfillment, and reverse logistics.

1. Transportation: The transportation component of distribution and logistics strategies deals with the movement of goods from one location to another. It involves selecting the most appropriate mode of transportation, whether it be by road, rail, air, or sea, based on factors such as cost, speed, reliability, and the nature of the products being transported.

- Road transportation: Road transportation is the most common mode used for shorter distances and ensures flexibility in terms of delivery schedules. Trucks, vans, and courier services are commonly employed in road transportation, offering door-to-door delivery options. Additionally, technologies such as GPS tracking and route optimization software have revolutionized the road transportation sector, enhancing efficiency and reducing costs.

- Rail transportation: Rail transportation is often chosen for long-distance shipping of bulk goods. It offers economies of scale, lower fuel costs, reduced traffic congestion, and lower carbon emissions compared to road transportation. Rail networks provide extensive coverage across countries and continents, connecting major manufacturing hubs to distribution centers and ports.

- Air transportation: Air transportation is preferred for time-sensitive and high-value products. It provides rapid delivery, global coverage, and the ability to reach remote locations. While air transportation can be costlier compared to other modes, advancements in technology have made it more accessible and efficient. Air freight hubs such as Hong Kong, Dubai, and Memphis have become critical nodes in the global supply chain.

- Sea transportation: Sea transportation is ideal for shipping large volumes of goods over long distances. It is cost-effective for bulk goods and offers the advantage of handling diverse cargo types, including dry goods, liquids, and oversized equipment. Containerization has revolutionized sea transportation, enabling easier handling, transport, and intermodal integration. Major ports like Shanghai, Singapore, Rotterdam, and Los Angeles are vital for global trade.

Efficient transportation management aims to minimize transit times, optimize routes, consolidate shipments, and reduce transportation costs. Emerging technologies such as route optimization software, autonomous vehicles, and real-time tracking systems enhance visibility and streamline the transportation process.

2. Warehousing: Warehousing is an integral part of distribution and logistics strategies as it involves the storage, handling, and management of inventory. The primary objective of warehousing is to ensure the availability of products when and where they are needed.

- Types of warehouses: Warehouses can be classified into various types based on their functionality. These include distribution centers, fulfillment centers, cross-docking facilities, bonded warehouses, temperature-controlled facilities, and more. Each type serves a specific purpose and caters to the needs of different industries. The selection of the appropriate warehouse type depends on factors such as product characteristics, demand patterns, proximity to customers, and overall supply chain strategy.

- Layout planning: Efficient warehouse layout planning optimizes space utilization, material flow, and order fulfillment processes. Factors such as product characteristics, storage requirements, throughput capacity, and picking strategies influence the layout design. Warehouse automation and robotics technologies help streamline operations, improve productivity, and increase storage density, providing significant competitive advantages.

- Inventory optimization: Inventory management within warehouses necessitates determining optimal stock levels, balancing stock inflow and outflow, and minimizing carrying costs. Techniques like ABC analysis, economic order quantity (EOQ), just-in-time (JIT) inventory replenishment, and safety stock calculations aid in maintaining the right inventory levels. Adoption of advanced technologies like RFID (radio frequency identification), barcode scanning, and inventory management systems enable real-time visibility and accurate inventory tracking.

- Order picking strategies: Order picking is a critical process within warehousing operations. Various strategies, such as batch picking, cluster picking, zone picking, and wave picking, are employed to enhance picking efficiency, reduce errors, and shorten order turnaround time. Robotic picking solutions and augmented reality technologies are transforming the picking process, improving speed, accuracy, and productivity.

- Technology solutions: Warehouse management systems (WMS) automate and optimize warehouse operations. These systems enable real-time inventory tracking, batch picking optimization, labor management, and integration with transportation systems for seamless order fulfillment. Robotics, artificial intelligence, and Internet of Things (IoT) technologies are increasingly integrated into warehousing operations to further enhance efficiency and responsiveness.

3. Inventory Management: Inventory is a critical aspect of distribution and logistics strategies as it helps balance supply and demand. Effective inventory management involves determining optimal stock levels, forecasting demand, monitoring stock movements, and implementing strategies to minimize stockouts or excess inventory.

  - Demand forecasting: Accurate demand forecasting is crucial for effective inventory management. Historical sales data, market trends, seasonality, and other factors are considered to forecast demand and plan inventory levels accordingly. Advanced predictive analytics models, machine learning algorithms, and big data analysis are increasingly utilized to improve forecasting accuracy.

  - Safety stock and lead time management: Safety stock acts as a buffer to protect against unforeseen fluctuations in demand or supply disruptions. Lead time management involves analyzing supply chain lead times to ensure that products are available in a timely manner to meet customer demands. Effective communication and collaboration with suppliers are essential to minimize lead time uncertainty.

  - Just-in-time (JIT) inventory replenishment: JIT inventory management aims to minimize inventory holding costs by receiving goods from suppliers exactly when they are needed for production or order fulfillment. This approach reduces storage requirements, improves cash flow, and facilitates lean supply chain practices. Collaboration with suppliers and implementation of electronic data interchange (EDI) systems support JIT replenishment.

  - Technology-enabled solutions: Advanced technologies such as RFID (radio frequency identification), barcode scanning, and inventory management software provide real-time visibility into inventory levels, streamline order fulfillment processes, and enable more accurate stock tracking. Cloud-based inventory management platforms allow for seamless integration and data sharing across the supply chain, ensuring accurate inventory replenishment and improved collaboration between stakeholders.

4. Order Fulfillment: Order fulfillment refers to the process of receiving and processing customer orders, picking and packing products, and delivering them to the customer within the agreed-upon timeframe. Efficient order fulfillment requires effective coordination between various stakeholders, including sales teams, warehouse staff, transportation providers, and technology platforms.

  - Order management systems (OMS): OMS platforms consolidate order information from multiple channels, enabling centralized order processing, inventory visibility, and real-time order tracking. Integration with warehouse management systems (WMS) ensures seamless order flow from receipt to delivery. OMS also supports order routing, allocation, and prioritization based on customer preferences, inventory availability, and delivery requirements.

- Streamlining picking and packing: Enhanced warehouse processes, such as optimized picking routes, automated picking technologies (such as pick-to-light or voice-guided picking), and efficient packing methods, contribute to faster order fulfillment and reduced order errors. The implementation of order consolidation techniques, such as batch picking and slotting optimization, enhances efficiency and boosts productivity.

- Last-mile delivery optimization: Last-mile delivery, the final leg of the logistics journey, plays a crucial role in customer satisfaction. Streamlined route planning, real-time tracking, and delivery scheduling optimizations help improve delivery efficiency and provide customers with better visibility. The utilization of route optimization software, delivery automation (including drones and autonomous vehicles), andreal-time communication with drivers enable faster and more accurate deliveries.

- Customer experience: The order fulfillment process directly impacts the customer experience. Efficient order processing, timely delivery, accurate order tracking, and seamless communication contribute to customer satisfaction. Providing multiple delivery options, such as same-day or next-day delivery, click-and-collect, or locker pickup, improves convenience and flexibility for customers.

- Returns and reverse logistics: Managing returns effectively is a crucial aspect of order fulfillment. Reverse logistics involves managing the flow of returned products, refurbishing or repairing them, and reintroducing them into the supply chain if possible. An efficient returns process helps maintain customer loyalty, reduce costs, and minimize environmental impact.

5. Technology Integration: The integration of technology solutions is a key enabler of efficient distribution and logistics strategies. Emerging technologies, such as artificial intelligence (AI), machine learning (ML), robotics, Internet of Things (IoT), and blockchain, have immense potential to streamline operations, enhance visibility, and drive innovation in the logistics industry.

- Advanced analytics and predictive modeling: Advanced analytics and predictive modeling techniques allow for improved demand forecasting, route optimization, inventory management, and customer segmentation. These technologies enable businesses to make data-driven decisions, optimize operations, and improve overall efficiency.

- Robotics and automation: Robotics and automation technologies have transformed various aspects of distribution and logistics. Automated material handling systems, robotics in picking and packing, autonomous vehicles for transportation, and automated guided vehicles (AGVs) in warehouses have significantly improved efficiency, accuracy, and speed. These technologies also help mitigate labor shortages and reduce manual errors.

- Internet of Things (IoT): IoT technologies have the potential to revolutionize supply chain visibility and monitoring. IoT devices, such as sensors, RFID tags, and GPS tracking, provide real-time data on the location, condition, and movement of products throughout the supply chain. This data enables proactive decision-making, improved inventory accuracy, and enhanced customer service.

- Blockchain: Blockchain technology offers enhanced transparency, security, and traceability in supply chain operations. It enables data sharing, authentication, and immutable records across multiple stakeholders, reducing fraud, increasing trust, and streamlining processes like track and trace, provenance verification, and contract management.

- Cloud-based systems: Cloud-based platforms and software solutions enable seamless integration and data sharing across the supply chain. Cloud computing provides scalability, accessibility, and real-time collaboration between different stakeholders. Warehouse management systems (WMS), transportation management systems (TMS), and order management systems (OMS) can be hosted on cloud platforms, facilitating real-time visibility and efficient decision-making.

Distribution and logistics strategies play a critical role in ensuring that products reach customers in a timely, cost-effective, and efficient manner. By leveraging transportation, warehousing, inventory management, order fulfillment, and technology solutions, businesses can optimize their supply chain operations and gain a competitive advantage in the market. Continuous evaluation, monitoring, and innovation are essential to adapt to evolving customer expectations, market dynamics, and technological advancements in the distribution and logistics landscape.

---

# 8. Technology and Innovation in Supply Chains

Technology and innovation play vital roles in the success of supply chains in today's rapidly changing business landscape. In this chapter, we will explore in-depth the various ways in which technology and innovation are revolutionizing supply chain management and bringing significant benefits to organizations.

1. Digitalization and Data Integration: The advent of digital technologies has paved the way for improved data collection, analysis, and integration across different stages of the supply chain. By utilizing technologies like cloud computing, big data analytics, and Internet of Things (IoT), organizations can gain real-time visibility into their supply chain operations and make data-driven decisions.

Cloud computing allows organizations to store and access a large amount of data securely, offering the flexibility to scale storage needs as the business grows. Advanced analytics on this data can provide insights into customer behavior, market trends, and identify areas for improvement within the supply chain. Additionally, IoT devices equipped with sensors and RFID technology can monitor the condition and location of assets, enabling organizations to track and trace goods throughout the supply chain.

Furthermore, digitalization enables organizations to obtain a holistic view of their supply chains, from procurement to delivery, allowing them to identify inefficiencies, optimize processes, and mitigate risks. By integrating data from multiple systems and stakeholders, organizations can enhance collaboration, eliminate information silos, and achieve greater supply chain transparency.

2. Automation and Robotics: Automation and robotics have transformed the way tasks are performed in supply chains. With the introduction of automated systems and robots, organizations can achieve higher accuracy, increased efficiency, and reduced labor costs in areas such as warehouse operations, order fulfillment, and transportation.

Automation technologies, such as autonomous guided vehicles (AGVs) and automated storage and retrieval systems (AS/RS), optimize warehouse operations by reducing manual errors, improving inventory accuracy, and increasing order fulfillment speed. AGVs can navigate through warehouses, picking and transporting goods, while AS/RS systems automate the storage and retrieval of pallets and containers. These technologies enable organizations to maximize space utilization and significantly reduce the time and effort required for routine warehouse tasks.

Furthermore, robotic process automation (RPA) streamlines administrative tasks, such as data entry and document processing, freeing up human resources to focus on more strategic activities. RPA can automate repetitive and rule-based processes, ensuring accurate and timely execution, thereby improving overall supply chain efficiency.

3. Artificial Intelligence and Machine Learning: Artificial Intelligence (AI) and Machine Learning (ML) algorithms have the potential to revolutionize supply chain planning and execution. These technologies can analyze vast amounts of data to identify patterns, optimize processes, predict demand, and enhance decision-making capabilities.

AI-powered demand forecasting models utilize historical data, market trends, and external factors to forecast future demand with higher accuracy. These forecasts allow organizations to proactively manage inventory levels, minimize stockouts, and reduce holding costs. ML algorithms can also automatically detect anomalies in supply chain data, enabling organizations to identify potential disruptions and implement mitigating actions promptly.

Furthermore, AI and ML algorithms can optimize transportation routes and logistics planning by considering various factors such as weather conditions, traffic congestion, and delivery time windows. By continuously analyzing data and making real-time adjustments, organizations can ensure efficient and cost-effective transportation operations.

4. Blockchain Technology: Blockchain technology is gaining traction in supply chain management due to its ability to provide transparency, traceability, and trust in transactions. With blockchain, organizations can securely track and verify the movement of goods, reduce fraud, and streamline processes like procurement, inventory management, and payments.

By recording transactions on an immutable and decentralized ledger, blockchain ensures data integrity and enables reliable auditing of supply chain activities. This technology can help organizations enhance supply chain traceability, particularly in industries like food and pharmaceuticals, where safety and compliance are critical. Blockchain also enables the development of smart contracts, automating and reducing the complexity of contract management between supply chain partners.

Smart contracts are self-executing contracts with the terms of the agreement written directly into the code. These contracts automatically trigger actions when predetermined conditions are met, eliminating the need for intermediaries and reducing transaction costs.

For example, a smart contract can release payment to a supplier once the delivery of goods is confirmed by IoT sensors.

5. Collaborative Platforms and Digital Marketplaces: Technology-enabled collaborative platforms and digital marketplaces are connecting suppliers, manufacturers, distributors, and customers in new and efficient ways. These platforms facilitate closer collaboration, streamlined communication, and improved coordination among supply chain partners.

Collaborative platforms enable real-time information sharing, fostering better collaboration and synchronization across the supply chain. They provide a centralized space for partners to exchange data, documents, and performance metrics, leading to improved visibility and enhanced decision-making capabilities. By analyzing shared data, organizations can identify potential bottlenecks, optimize inventory levels, and collectively respond to disruptions in a timely manner.

Digital marketplaces, on the other hand, connect buyers and sellers, allowing organizations to access a broader range of suppliers and customers, increasing market reach and product/service offerings. These marketplaces provide greater transparency and facilitate seamless transactions through features such as rating systems, reviews, and secure payment gateways. By leveraging digital marketplaces, organizations can expand their network and discover new business opportunities beyond their traditional customer base.

6. Innovation in Last-Mile Delivery: Last-mile delivery, the final step in the supply chain, is witnessing significant technological advancements. Companies are exploring innovative solutions such as drone delivery, autonomous vehicles, and crowd-sharing platforms to optimize delivery processes, reduce costs, and enhance customer experience.

Drone delivery offers the potential to overcome challenges related to traffic congestion, remote locations, and speed of delivery. With the ability to bypass traditional transportation routes, drones can deliver packages faster and at lower costs. Companies like Amazon and UPS have been piloting drone delivery services in select areas, demonstrating the potential of this technology.

Autonomous vehicles, including self-driving trucks and delivery robots, are being tested to optimize last-mile operations, improve efficiency, and reduce both emissions and labor costs. Self-driving trucks can navigate predefined routes, reducing the need for human drivers and enabling continuous operations. Delivery robots, on the other hand, can navigate sidewalks and safely deliver packages to customers' doorsteps. These innovations have the potential to revolutionize the last-mile delivery landscape, making it more efficient, cost-effective, and environmentally friendly.

Crowd-sharing platforms allow individuals to monetize their unused capacity, such as trunk space in their vehicles. These platforms connect businesses with independent drivers who can perform last-mile deliveries, offering flexible and cost-effective solutions. Delivery optimization algorithms match the proximity and availability of drivers with delivery requests, ensuring efficient and timely completion of deliveries. Furthermore, these innovative solutions are often supported by real-time tracking and notifications, enhancing the visibility and traceability of goods during the last mile.

7. Supply Chain Analytics: Advanced analytics tools enable organizations to extract meaningful insights from the vast amount of supply chain data available. By harnessing analytics, organizations can identify trends, optimize their operations, and make proactive decisions to improve overall supply chain performance.

Predictive analytics leverages historical and real-time data to forecast future demand, identify potential bottlenecks, optimize inventory levels, and enhance supply chain responsiveness. These forecasts help organizations align their production and distribution capabilities more accurately and efficiently, leading to improved customer satisfaction and reduced costs.

Prescriptive analytics takes it a step further, providing organizations with data-driven recommendations on how to improve processes, mitigate risks, and optimize their supply chain strategies. Byanalyzing various "what-if" scenarios, organizations can evaluate the potential impact of different decisions and choose the best course of action.

Descriptive analytics provides organizations with a retrospective view of their supply chain performance. By analyzing historical data, organizations can identify trends, patterns, and outliers, allowing them to understand the root causes of issues and make informed decisions for continuous improvement.

Visualization tools and dashboards provide a visual representation of supply chain data, making it easier for organizations to understand complex information and identify areas for improvement. These tools allow for real-time monitoring of key performance indicators (KPIs), enabling organizations to track their performance and take immediate action when deviations occur.

8. Sustainability and Green Supply Chain: Technology and innovation are also driving the adoption of sustainable practices and the development of green supply chains. As organizations become more focused on social responsibility and environmental sustainability, technology plays a crucial role in enabling them to reduce their carbon footprint and implement sustainable practices.

Optimization algorithms can help organizations minimize transportation costs and reduce emissions by optimizing route planning, load consolidation, and vehicle scheduling. By considering factors such as distance, traffic, and fuel efficiency, these algorithms can generate optimal transportation plans that reduce both costs and environmental impact.

Furthermore, the use of IoT sensors in logistics and transportation can monitor energy consumption, track carbon emissions, and identify areas for improvement. Organizations can use this data to establish sustainability benchmarks, set targets, and implement measures to reduce energy usage and emissions.

In addition, technology-enabled traceability systems, such as RFID and blockchain, can ensure transparency and accountability in supply chains, allowing organizations to identify and mitigate risks related to environmental compliance and ethical sourcing. By tracking the origin of materials and ensuring compliance with environmental regulations, organizations can ensure the sustainability and ethicality of their supply chains.

Overall, technology and innovation have revolutionized supply chain management, bringing cost savings, efficiency improvements, and sustainability benefits to organizations. By embracing these advancements, organizations can gain a competitive edge, enhance customer satisfaction, and future-proof their supply chains in an increasingly digital and interconnected world.

---

# 9. Sustainability and Ethical Considerations

In today's rapidly changing world, businesses face increasing pressure to adopt sustainable and ethical practices throughout their operations. Sustainability is the ability of a business to meet its present needs without compromising the needs of future generations. It entails considering the environmental, social, and economic impacts of business decisions. Ethical considerations, on the other hand, revolve around conducting business in a morally responsible manner, fostering trust and integrity with stakeholders.

1. The Importance of Sustainability:

Now more than ever, sustainability is crucial for the long-term success of any business. Environmental issues such as climate change, resource depletion, and pollution have become urgent concerns globally. Consumers, investors, and governments are demanding greater transparency and accountability from companies to minimize their negative impact on the environment. By incorporating sustainable practices, businesses can reduce their carbon footprint, minimize waste, and contribute positively to the communities in which they operate.

Sustainability goes beyond environmental considerations. It also encompasses social and economic dimensions. Social sustainability involves respecting human rights, promoting fair and safe working conditions, and contributing to the well-being of communities. Economic sustainability entails creating long-term value for shareholders, fostering economic growth, and ensuring financial stability.

2. Ethical Considerations in the Supply Chain:

Supply chains have transformed into complex, global networks involving multiple stakeholders. Ensuring ethical practices throughout the supply chain is essential to avoid reputational damage and legal consequences. Factors such as fair labor practices, human rights, and responsible sourcing of raw materials are integral to maintaining an ethical supply chain.

One critical aspect of ethical supply chains is addressing labor practices. Companies must ensure fair wages, reasonable working hours, and safe working conditions for all employees, including those at supplier facilities. Child labor, forced labor, and discrimination should be actively combated, and engagement with suppliers should involve close oversight and continuous improvement efforts.

Beyond labor practices, responsible sourcing of raw materials is essential. This involves assessing and monitoring the environmental and social impacts associated with raw material extraction, as well as the welfare of communities affected by these activities. Transparent and traceable supply chains play a vital role in preventing the use of conflict minerals, protecting indigenous rights, and fostering sustainable resource management.

3. Implementing Sustainable Supply Chain Management:

Integrating sustainability into supply chain management requires a comprehensive approach:

   a. Evaluate and Select Suppliers: Assess suppliers based on their environmental and ethical records, with a preference for those who prioritize sustainability practices. Implement supplier evaluation and selection systems that consider sustainability criteria alongside quality, cost, and delivery performance.

   b. Green Procurement: Source environmentally friendly materials and incorporate sustainability criteria into procurement decisions. Consider factors like energy consumption, greenhouse gas emissions, labor standards, and the overall lifecycle impact of products. By actively engaging suppliers in sustainable product development, companies can drive innovation and promote environmentally friendly alternatives.

   c. Reduce Carbon Footprint: Optimize transportation routes, promote energy-efficient practices in manufacturing and logistics, and explore alternative energy sources to reduce greenhouse gas emissions. Collaborate with logistics providers and invest in greener transportation options where feasible. Adopting circular economy principles, such as remanufacturing and recycling, can also help reduce emissions and conserve resources.

   d. Waste Reduction and Recycling: Implement waste management programs, encourage recycling, and explore circular economy models to minimize waste generation. Engage suppliers in initiatives to reduce packaging waste and encourage the use of recyclable materials. By adopting closed-loop systems, businesses can transform waste into valuable resources, contributing to both environmental and economic sustainability.

   e. Collaboration and Transparency: Work closely with suppliers, customers, and other stakeholders to foster collaboration and transparency in sustainable initiatives. Sharing sustainability goals, best practices, and progress updates can strengthen partnerships and drive collective progress towards sustainability. Engaging with suppliers through capacity-building programs and knowledge sharing platforms can also help improve sustainability practices throughout the supply chain.

4. Stakeholder Engagement and Reporting:

Engaging stakeholders, such as employees, customers, communities, and investors, is essential for successful sustainability initiatives. It creates a sense of shared responsibility and fosters a stronger commitment towards sustainability goals. Collaboration with stakeholders can help identify and prioritize sustainability issues, generate innovative solutions, and communicate progress effectively. Additionally, transparent reporting of sustainability initiatives and performance metrics demonstrates accountability and builds trust among stakeholders.

Companies can engage stakeholders through various means, such as regular communication, consultation forums, and participation in multi-stakeholder initiatives. By incorporating stakeholder input into decision-making processes, businesses gain valuable insights, ensure inclusivity, and strengthen their social license to operate. Reporting on sustainability performance, using widely recognized frameworks like the Global Reporting Initiative (GRI) or Sustainability Accounting Standards Board (SASB), provides stakeholders with measurable indicators to assess a company's sustainability progress.

5. Ethical Challenges and Solutions:

Implementing ethical practices in the supply chain can pose challenges due to differing cultural norms, diverse supply chain networks, and limited visibility into lower-tier suppliers. However, companies can address these challenges by:

a. Code of Conduct: Establish a comprehensive code of conduct for suppliers, encompassing ethical practices and expectations. Clearly communicate these expectations and provide guidance on responsible conduct. Regularly review and update the code of conduct to reflect changing social, environmental, and legal landscapes.

b. Auditing and Monitoring: Conduct regular audits and assessments of suppliers to ensure compliance with ethical standards. Implement monitoring systems to track supplier performance and take corrective actions when necessary. Third-party audits and certifications can provide an independent verification of suppliers' ethical practices.

c. Collaboration and Training: Collaborate with suppliers to improve their understanding of ethical practices and provide training on responsible supply chain management. Support suppliers in implementing necessary changes and building their capacity for ethical operations. By fostering long-term relationships with suppliers based on mutual trust and shared values, companies have a better chance of driving sustainable and ethical improvements.

d. Certification and Recognition: Encourage suppliers to obtain certifications for environmental and ethical practices, enabling recognition for their efforts. Recognizing suppliers that meet or exceed ethical standards can incentivize positive change throughout the supply chain. Participating in industry initiatives, such as the Responsible Business Alliance (RBA) or Sustainable Apparel Coalition (SAC), can provide guidance, tools, and collaboration opportunities for responsible sourcing.

6. Emerging Trends and Future Outlook:

Sustainability and ethical considerations will only grow in importance as businesses strive to be socially responsible and meet evolving consumer expectations. As technology advances, companies can leverage innovations such as blockchain technology for enhanced transparency and traceability in the supply chain. Blockchain can help verify and record ethical practices, providing greater assurance to consumers and stakeholders. Additionally, circular economy principles, renewable energy sources, and responsible sourcing will play an increasingly significant role in creating sustainable and ethical supply chains.

Embracing a circular economy, where resources are used efficiently, waste is minimized, and products have longer lifecycles, enables a shift towards a more sustainable future. Renewable energy sources, such as solar and wind power, are becoming more accessible and affordable, offering opportunities for businesses to reduce their carbon footprint and contribute to mitigating climate change. Responsible sourcing not only helps protect the environment and promote social well-being but also ensures the long-term availability of essential resources for future generations.

In conclusion, incorporating sustainability and ethical considerations into supply chain management is imperative for businesses to thrive in the future. By embracing responsible practices, companies can mitigate risks, improve their brand image, attract loyal customers, and contribute to a better world for generations tocome. However, it is important to note that implementing sustainable and ethical practices is not without its challenges. Some of the key challenges businesses may face include:

1. Cost considerations: Implementing sustainable and ethical practices can sometimes require upfront investments in new technologies, training programs, and certifications. This can put a strain on a company's budget, especially for small and medium-sized enterprises. However, it is important to view these investments as long-term strategies that can lead to cost savings and increased competitiveness in the future.

2. Complexity of supply chains: Supply chains today are complex and global, with multiple tiers of suppliers. This complexity can make it challenging for businesses to have full visibility

and control over every aspect of their supply chain, including ethical practices. Many companies rely on third-party audits and certifications to ensure compliance, but these measures are not infallible. It requires ongoing monitoring and collaboration with suppliers to address any issues that may arise.

3. Limited resources and knowledge: Some businesses, particularly smaller ones, may lack the necessary resources and knowledge to effectively implement sustainable and ethical practices. They may not have dedicated sustainability or CSR departments, and may struggle to keep up with rapidly evolving regulations and market trends. In these cases, seeking external expertise and collaborating with industry associations and organizations can help bridge the knowledge gap and provide practical guidance.

Despite these challenges, there are numerous benefits to integrating sustainability and ethics into the supply chain. Some of these benefits include:

1. Enhanced reputation and brand value: Consumers are increasingly conscious of the environmental and social impact of the products and services they consume. By demonstrating a commitment to sustainability and ethics, businesses can enhance their reputation and differentiate themselves from their competitors. This can lead to increased customer loyalty and a positive brand image.

2. Increased operational efficiency: Many sustainable practices, such as energy efficiency, waste reduction, and responsible sourcing, can also lead to cost savings and increased operational efficiency. For example, optimizing transportation routes can reduce fuel costs, while recycling and reusing materials can minimize waste disposal expenses. These efficiency gains can contribute to the bottom line and improve overall business performance.

3. Access to new markets and customers: As sustainability becomes a priority for consumers, businesses that can demonstrate their commitment to sustainability and ethical practices will have an advantage in accessing new markets and attracting environmentally and socially conscious customers. This can lead to increased sales and market share.

4. Regulatory compliance: Governments around the world are implementing stricter regulations and standards related to sustainability and ethical practices. By proactively incorporating these practices into their supply chain, businesses can ensure compliance with these regulations and avoid potential legal and financial risks.

In conclusion, sustainability and ethical considerations are no longer optional for businesses. They are a necessity in today's global marketplace. By integrating sustainable and ethical practices throughout the supply chain, businesses can mitigate risks, improve their reputation, access new markets, and contribute to the well-being of the planet and future generations. It requires a proactive and collaborative approach, close engagement with suppliers and stakeholders, and ongoing monitoring and improvement efforts.

---

# 10. Risk Management in the Supply Chain

Introduction:
Risk management is an essential aspect of supply chain management as it ensures the smooth functioning and resilience of the supply chain network. In today's complex and interconnected business environment, supply chains are exposed to various risks that can disrupt operations and impact business performance. This chapter explores the different types of risks encountered in the supply chain and provides insights into effective risk management strategies.

1. Identifying Risks:
Supply chains are vulnerable to a wide range of risks, both internal and external. Internal risks can include operational inefficiencies, poor inventory management, lack of communication within the supply chain network, and inadequate risk awareness within organizations. External risks, on the other hand, can stem from natural disasters such as earthquakes, hurricanes, floods, or fires, geopolitical uncertainties, economic fluctuations and recessions, supplier disruptions, regulatory changes, trade disputes, piracy, counterfeit products, technological disruptions, cyber attacks, and terrorist activities. By conducting a comprehensive risk assessment, organizations can gain a better understanding of their risk exposure and vulnerabilities.

2. Assessing Risks:
Once risks are identified, it is important to assess their potential impact and likelihood. Quantitative and qualitative risk assessment techniques help in evaluating the consequences associated with each risk. Quantitative analysis involves assigning numeric values to the likelihood and impact of risks, enabling organizations to prioritize and allocate resources efficiently. It involves statistical analysis, historical data analysis, simulation modeling, and computational methods. Qualitative analysis, on the other hand, considers expert opinions and judgment to evaluate risks that are difficult to quantify. Techniques such as risk mapping, brainstorming, scenario analysis, and probability assessments can be used effectively. Through risk mapping, organizations can visually represent different risks on a chart and assess areas of high concentration. Scenario analysis involves developing hypothetical situations and evaluating their impact on the supply chain to evaluate risks. The probability assessments help organizations understand the likelihood of risk occurrence, enabling informed decision-making. By combining both quantitative and

qualitative approaches, organizations can gain a holistic view of their risk landscape.

3. Mitigating Risks:

Risk mitigation involves implementing strategies and measures to reduce the likelihood and impact of identified risks. Organizations can adopt various approaches such as diversifying supplier networks to avoid overreliance on a single source, developing robust supplier selection and evaluation processes, implementing effective quality control mechanisms, developing backup plans and alternative sources of supply, securing insurance coverage to mitigate financial risks, implementing robust cybersecurity measures such as firewalls, encryption, and intrusion detection systems to protect against cyber threats, establishing effective crisis management protocols to respond to disruptions swiftly, and conducting regular procurement audits to ensure compliance with regulations, policies, and ethical standards. Additionally, integrating sustainability practices into the supply chain helps mitigate environmental risks and ensures long-term viability. Collaborative relationships with suppliers and partners can also help in sharing risks and jointly developing mitigation strategies. By engaging in proactive risk management, organizations can reduce their vulnerability to disruptions and enhance the overall resilience of their supply chain network.

4. Collaborative Risk Management:

Given the interconnected nature of supply chains, it is important for organizations to engage in collaborative risk management with their key stakeholders. This includes sharing information, conducting joint risk assessments, and collaboratively developing risk mitigation strategies. Collaboration is especially crucial in industries where suppliers are critical to the success of the organization, such as automotive or aerospace sectors. By establishing strong relationships and communication channels with suppliers, customers, and logistics providers, organizations can enhance their ability to identify and address risks collectively. Collaboration fosters trust, transparency, and enhances the overall resilience of the supply chain network. Joint risk management initiatives can include supplier audits, joint training sessions, joint planning exercises, and sharing best practices.

5. Monitoring and Response:

Risks in the supply chain are dynamic and constantly evolving. Therefore, it is crucial to continuously monitor the environment for new risks or changes in existing risks. This involves setting up early warning systems to detect potential disruptions, establishing key performance indicators (KPIs) to track risk-related metrics, and implementing effective response plans to address any disruptions or threats. Organizations can leverage technology and data analytics to monitor supply chain operations in real-time, enabling proactive risk management. Regular communication, transparency, and real-time data sharing with stakeholders enable organizations to proactively manage risks and respond swiftly to emerging challenges. By implementing effective monitoring and response mechanisms, organizations can minimize the impact of disruptions and maintain business continuity.

6. Continuous Improvement:

Risk management in the supply chain is an ongoing process that requires continuous improvement. Organizations should regularly review and evaluate their risk management strategies, learn from past incidents or near misses, and adapt their approaches to address emerging risks. Through post-event analysis, organizations can identify areas for improvement, revise risk mitigation plans, and refine their risk response capabilities. Regular training and awareness programs also help in developing a proactive risk management culture within the organization. Continuous improvement ensures that the supply chain remains robust and resilient in the face of evolving risk landscapes. Organizations can leverage emerging technologies such as artificial intelligence, machine learning, and predictive analytics to strengthen risk management capabilities. These technologies enable organizations to detect patterns, predict potential risks, and make data-driven decisions.

Conclusion:

Effectively managing risks in the supply chain is vital for organizations to safeguard their operations and maintain a competitive edge. By identifying, assessing, mitigating, and continuously monitoring risks, companies can enhance their ability to respond to disruptions, protect their reputation, and minimize the financial impact of supply chain risks. Embracing a proactive and collaborative approach to risk management enables organizations to build resilient supply chain networks that can withstand uncertainties and deliver value to customers. With the ever-changing risk landscape, organizations must adapt and evolve their risk management strategies to ensure the long-term success of their supply chains. By integrating robust risk management practices into the supply chain, organizations can thrive in challenging environments and strengthen their position in the market.

---

# 11. Demand Forecasting and Planning

Demand forecasting and planning are crucial elements of effective supply chain management. They involve predicting customer demand for products or services and aligning production and inventory levels accordingly. By accurately forecasting demand, businesses can optimize their supply chain operations, reduce costs, and improve customer satisfaction.

1. The Importance of Demand Forecasting:
Demand forecasting plays a pivotal role in supply chain management as it allows businesses to anticipate future customer demand patterns. This prediction is based on a comprehensive analysis of historical data, market trends, customer behavior, economic conditions, and other relevant factors. It helps in strategic decision-making, such as capacity planning, production scheduling, and inventory management. A reliable demand forecast ensures that organizations have the right quantity of products available at the right time, reducing stockouts or excess inventory levels.

2. Factors Influencing Demand:
To achieve accurate demand forecasting, businesses need to consider a wide range of factors that can influence customer demand. These factors include economic conditions, consumer behavior, seasonality, competitors' activities, promotional campaigns, emerging technology trends, regulatory changes, and external events. By analyzing these factors, businesses can make more accurate predictions and respond effectively to changes in demand patterns.

2.1 Economic Conditions:
Economic conditions, such as GDP growth, inflation rates, interest rates, and employment levels, can have a significant impact on consumer spending patterns and overall demand. During periods of economic downturn, consumers tend to be more cautious with their spending, leading to a decrease in demand for non-essential products. Conversely, during economic upswings, consumer confidence and spending tend to increase, boosting demand.

2.2 Consumer Behavior:
Understanding consumer behavior is crucial for accurate demand forecasting. Factors such as demographics, lifestyle changes, purchasing habits, and preferences greatly influence

customer demand. For instance, an aging population might lead to an increased demand for healthcare products and services, while changing consumer preferences for eco-friendly products can drive demand for sustainable alternatives.

## 2.3 Seasonality:

Seasonal fluctuations impact demand for many products. Retailers often experience increased demand during holiday seasons or specific periods like summer or winter. Understanding these patterns allows businesses to adjust their production levels and inventory accordingly, ensuring sufficient stock during peak periods and reducing excess inventory during slower periods.

## 2.4 Competitors' Activities:

Monitoring competitors' activities is essential for demand forecasting. Changes in their pricing strategies, product launches, promotional campaigns, or expansion plans may influence customer demand. By staying informed about competitors' actions, businesses can anticipate potential shifts in the market and adjust their own strategies accordingly.

## 2.5 Promotional Campaigns:

Promotions and marketing campaigns can significantly impact demand. Offering discounts, coupons, or loyalty programs can attract customers and drive higher sales. However, businesses need to carefully assess the impact of different promotional activities to avoid overestimating demand and facing inventory management challenges.

## 2.6 Emerging Technology Trends:

Advancements in technology can create new opportunities and influence customer demand. For example, the rise of e-commerce has revolutionized the retail industry, leading to changes in consumer purchasing behavior, such as increased demand for online shopping and home delivery services. Monitoring technological trends allows businesses to proactively adapt their supply chain strategies to cater to evolving customer demands.

## 2.7 Regulatory Changes:

Changes in regulations can have a significant impact on demand for certain products or industries. New safety standards, certifications, or environmental regulations may require businesses to modify their product offerings or production processes, affecting both supply and demand. Being aware of these regulatory changes ahead of time ensures businesses can adjust their operations proactively.

## 2.8 External Events:

External events, such as natural disasters, political instability, or global pandemics, can have an immediate and substantial impact on demand. These events can disrupt supply chains, create sudden spikes or drops in demand, and alter customer behavior. Businesses need to incorporate contingency plans into their demand forecasting and planning processes to handle such unforeseen circumstances.

## 3. Demand Forecasting Techniques:
Demand forecasting involves both qualitative and quantitative methods. These techniques help assess demand based on historical data and other market insights.

### 3.1 Qualitative Methods:
Qualitative methods rely on expert opinions, market research, surveys, and subjective judgments to forecast demand. These methods are particularly useful in situations where historical data is limited, unreliable, or non-existent, such as when launching a new product or entering emerging markets. Qualitative methods include the Delphi method, market research, and expert panels.

### 3.2 Quantitative Methods:
Quantitative methods use historical data and various statistical models to forecast demand accurately. These methods are suitable when reliable historical data is available. Common quantitative forecasting techniques include time series analysis, regression analysis, moving averages, exponential smoothing, and causal modeling. These methods evaluate patterns and trends in the historical data, allowing businesses to project demand into the future.

#### 3.2.1 Time Series Analysis:
Time series analysis is a statistical technique that examines historical data to identify patterns and trends over time. This method helps detect seasonality, trends, and cyclical patterns, enabling businesses to make informed predictions based on past data. Time series analysis can be conducted using various models, such as moving averages, exponential smoothing, or ARIMA models.

#### 3.2.2 Regression Analysis:
Regression analysis helps businesses understand the relationship between the dependent variable (demand) and independent variables (factors influencing demand) by fitting a regression equation. It uses historical data to estimate the parameters and forecast future demand based on changes in the independent variables. Regression analysis allows businesses to quantify the impact of different factors on demand and make more accurate predictions.

#### 3.2.3 Moving Averages:
Moving averages calculate the average demand over a specific period, smoothing out short-term fluctuations and highlighting long-term trends. It is commonly used for demand forecasting when seasonality is not significant or when data is noisy. Moving averages provide a simple yet effective way to predict future demand based on historical averages.

#### 3.2.4 Exponential Smoothing:

Exponential smoothing is a widely used forecasting method that assigns exponentially decreasing weights to past observations, giving more importance to recent data. This technique is suitable when there is no significant seasonality or when demand patterns exhibit constant growth or decay. Exponential smoothing provides more accurate predictions by considering recent trends and discarding irrelevant historical data.

3.2.5 Causal Modeling:

Causal modeling involves identifying cause-and-effect relationships between demand and various factors, such as pricing, promotional activities, competitors' actions, or economic indicators. This method uses historical data to estimate the impact of each factor on demand and forecast future demand based on anticipated changes in these factors. Causal modeling allows businesses to simulate different scenarios and evaluate the effects of strategic decisions on demand.

4. Demand Planning and Collaboration:

Demand planning involves developing a detailed plan for meeting forecasted demand by aligning procurement, production, and distribution activities. It requires collaboration between various departments within an organization, such as sales, marketing, operations, finance, and supply chain management. Cross-functional collaboration allows for a holistic approach to demand planning, enabling teams to consider different perspectives and expertise. By working together, teams can ensure that the supply chain is well-prepared to handle anticipated demand fluctuations and effectively respond to changes in customer requirements.

4.1 Sales and Marketing Collaboration:

Sales and marketing teams play a crucial role in demand forecasting and planning. They provide insights into promotions, sales trends, new product launches, customer feedback, and upcoming campaigns. By collaborating closely with these teams, businesses canleverage their market knowledge and customer insights to improve the accuracy of demand forecasts. Sales and marketing teams can provide valuable input on potential changes in customer behavior, competitive dynamics, and market trends. This information can then be integrated into the demand forecasting and planning processes to ensure that production and inventory levels align with expected demand.

4.2 Operations Collaboration:

Close collaboration between the demand planning team and operations team is essential to ensure the successful execution of demand plans. The operations team is responsible for translating the forecasted demand into production requirements, capacity planning, and inventory management. By working together, these teams can optimize production schedules, allocate resources efficiently, and minimize production and distribution costs. Regular communication and collaboration ensure that demand forecasts are translated into actionable plans that meet customer requirements while maintaining operational efficiency.

4.3 Finance Collaboration:
The finance team plays a critical role in demand planning by providing financial insights and resources to support production and inventory decisions. They help assess the financial implications of different demand scenarios, evaluate the profitability of products or services, set pricing strategies, and allocate financial resources effectively. Collaboration between the finance team and demand planning team ensures that financial considerations are integrated into the demand planning process, enabling businesses to make informed decisions that align with their financial goals.

4.4 Supply Chain Collaboration:
Collaboration across the entire supply chain is crucial for effective demand planning. This includes collaboration with suppliers, distributors, and logistics partners. By sharing demand forecasts and insights with supply chain partners, businesses can improve supply chain visibility, enhance inventory management, and reduce lead times. Collaborative relationships with suppliers and distributors allow for faster responses to changes in demand, enabling businesses to meet customer requirements more effectively and reduce the risk of stockouts or excess inventory levels.

5. Benefits of Effective Demand Forecasting and Planning:
Implementing effective demand forecasting and planning processes can provide several benefits to businesses:

5.1 Improved Customer Service:
Accurate demand forecasting helps businesses ensure that they have sufficient stock levels to meet customer demand. By avoiding stockouts or excess inventory, businesses can improve order fulfillment, reduce lead times, and enhance customer satisfaction. Meeting customer demand promptly and reliably contributes to positive customer experiences and builds loyalty.

5.2 Reduced Costs:
Demand forecasting and planning help optimize production, inventory, and distribution levels. By aligning supply with demand, businesses can minimize both excess inventory costs and stockouts, reducing holding costs and avoiding lost sales. Effective demand planning also enables businesses to optimize production schedules, reduce waste, and streamline supply chain operations, leading to cost savings.

5.3 Enhanced Operational Efficiency:
By accurately forecasting demand, businesses can plan production and procurement activities more effectively. This leads to better utilization of resources, improved production scheduling, and increased efficiency. With the right balance between supply and demand, businesses can reduce operational bottlenecks and optimize their supply chain processes.

5.4 Strategic Decision-Making:
Demand forecasting and planning provide valuable insights into future demand patterns, market trends, and customer behavior. This information enables businesses to make informed strategic decisions, such as new product launches, market expansions, capacity planning, and investment decisions. Accurate demand forecasting empowers businesses to allocate resources efficiently and proactively respond to changes in customer requirements or market dynamics.

5.5 Minimized Risk:
Effective demand forecasting and planning help businesses minimize the risk of stockouts, excess inventory, or obsolescence. By having a well-balanced supply and demand alignment, businesses are better prepared to handle unexpected fluctuations in demand or external events. Contingency plans developed as part of demand planning enable businesses to mitigate risks and quickly adapt to changing market conditions.

In conclusion, demand forecasting and planning are essential elements of successful supply chain management. By accurately predicting customer demand, businesses can optimize their production, procurement, and distribution strategies. This leads to improved customer service, reduced costs, enhanced operational efficiency, and better strategic decision-making. Effective demand forecasting and planning enable businesses to stay competitive, responsive to market demands, and maximize their overall supply chain performance.

————————

# 12. Lean and Agile Principles in Supply Chain

In today's dynamic business environment, supply chains need to be agile and adaptable to stay competitive. This is where the principles of lean and agile come into play. Lean and agile practices help organizations optimize their supply chain processes, reduce waste, and respond quickly to changes in customer demands.

Lean principles focus on maximizing value and eliminating waste throughout the supply chain. It emphasizes continuous improvement, creating flow, and establishing pull-based systems. By applying lean principles, organizations can minimize inventory levels, reduce lead times, and improve overall efficiency.

One of the key aspects of lean supply chain management is the identification and elimination of waste. Waste can manifest in various forms such as overproduction, excess inventory, defects, unnecessary transportation, motion, waiting time, and underutilized talent or resources. By eliminating these wastes, organizations can streamline their operations and save costs.

To effectively identify waste and implement lean principles, organizations often utilize tools and methodologies such as Value Stream Mapping (VSM), Kaizen events, 5S (Sort, Set in Order, Shine, Standardize, Sustain), and Just-in-Time (JIT) production. Value Stream Mapping helps visualize the entire supply chain process and identify areas of improvement, while Kaizen events bring together cross-functional teams to brainstorm and implement continuous improvement initiatives. The 5S methodology focuses on workplace organization and standardization to increase efficiency and reduce waste, while JIT production aims to produce and deliver products in the exact quantities and at the precise time they are needed.

Agile principles, on the other hand, emphasize flexibility and responsiveness in the supply chain. Agile supply chains are characterized by their ability to quickly adapt to changes in demand, customer preferences, or market conditions. This involves collaborating closely with suppliers, customers, and other stakeholders, as well as leveraging technology for real-time information sharing.

To implement agile principles in supply chain management, organizations need to focus on a few key strategies. Firstly, they should adopt a customer-centric approach, aiming to understand and meet the real needs of their customers. By doing so, organizations can reduce lead times and respond faster to changing customer demand. This can be achieved through practices such as demand sensing, customer segmentation, and personalized product offerings.

Secondly, organizations should prioritize cross-functional collaboration and information sharing. This helps to break down silos within the organization and enables a holistic view of the supply chain. By fostering collaboration among different departments, organizations can reduce bottlenecks, improve overall efficiency, and enhance decision-making processes. Collaborative planning, forecasting, and replenishment (CPFR) is one approach that promotes joint planning and coordination with key supply chain partners.

Another crucial aspect of lean and agile supply chain management is the use of technology and data analytics. Organizations can leverage technology solutions such as advanced analytics, cloud computing, automation, and Artificial Intelligence (AI) to gather and analyze data in real-time. This helps in identifying patterns, making informed decisions, and proactively responding to changes in the supply chain. Integrated systems and digital platforms enable seamless information flow across the supply chain, facilitating faster communication and real-time visibility.

Additionally, organizations should focus on continuous improvement and regularly review their supply chain processes. This involves measuring and monitoring key performance indicators (KPIs) to identify areas for improvement. By embracing a culture of continuous learning, organizations can adapt their supply chain strategies and practices to meet evolving market demands. Kaizen (continuous improvement), Total Quality Management (TQM), and Six Sigma are methodologies commonly employed to drive continuous improvement initiatives in the supply chain.

Moreover, risk management plays a critical role in lean and agile supply chains. Organizations need to proactively identify, assess, and mitigate potential risks to ensure operational resilience. This includes supply disruptions, environmental impacts, geopolitical risks, and regulatory changes. By having contingency plans, alternate supply sources, and robust risk assessment processes, organizations can minimize the impact of disruptions and quickly recover.

Furthermore, sustainability is becoming increasingly important in supply chain management. Lean and agile practices can contribute to sustainable supply chains by reducing waste, optimizing resource utilization, and minimizing environmental impacts. Organizations can adopt environmentally-friendly practices such as eco-design, reverse logistics, and responsible sourcing to align their supply chains with sustainability goals.

In conclusion, lean and agile principles are vital for effective supply chain management in today's fast-paced business environment. By adopting lean practices, organizations can eliminate waste and improve efficiency, while agile principles enable quick adaptation to changes in customer demand and market conditions. By embracing these principles, organizations can build resilient, sustainable, and competitive supply chains that can thrive in a rapidly changing marketplace. The integration of technology, cross-functional collaboration, continuous improvement, risk management, and sustainability are essential components in achieving lean and agile supply chains.

---

# 13. Performance Metrics and KPIs

Effective supply chain management is a complex and multifaceted endeavor that requires organizations to have a thorough understanding of the performance metrics and key performance indicators (KPIs) that allow them to measure and assess the success of their supply chain operations. These metrics provide vital insights into the effectiveness and efficiency of supply chain processes, enabling organizations to make informed decisions, identify areas of improvement, and drive overall supply chain performance. In this chapter, we will delve deep into the importance of performance metrics and KPIs in supply chain management and discuss some commonly used metrics.

1. On-time Delivery Performance: On-time delivery performance is a critical metric that measures the percentage of orders that are delivered to the customer on time, as promised. It serves as an essential indicator of customer satisfaction and plays a crucial role in maintaining a reliable supply chain. Organizations can track on-time delivery performance by comparing planned delivery dates to actual delivery dates. This metric helps identify potential delays and bottlenecks in the supply chain, allowing for proactive measures to ensure timely deliveries. Additionally, it enables organizations to assess their performance against customer expectations and contractual agreements.

2. Order Accuracy: The order accuracy metric measures the percentage of orders that are fulfilled accurately, without any errors or discrepancies. It reflects an organization's ability to process orders effectively and meet customer expectations. Order accuracy can be evaluated by comparing the quantity and specifications of ordered items with those delivered. High order accuracy ensures customer satisfaction, minimizes returns, and reduces costs associated with order corrections. Organizations can leverage this metric to identify any gaps in the order fulfillment process and implement corrective actions to enhance accuracy.

3. Inventory Turnover: Inventory turnover is a measure of how quickly an organization sells and replaces its inventory. It is calculated by dividing the cost of goods sold by the average inventory value. A higher inventory turnover ratio indicates efficient inventory management and lower carrying costs. Organizations can monitor inventory turnover to optimize inventory levels, minimize stockouts, and avoid excess inventory. This metric helps strike a balance between customer demand and optimal inventory levels. Furthermore, analyzing

inventory turnover trends over time provides valuable insights into demand patterns, allowing organizations to forecast more accurately and plan their production accordingly.

4. Fill Rate: Fill rate is a critical metric that measures the percentage of customer demand that is fulfilled from available inventory. It helps track an organization's ability to meet customer requirements in a timely manner and avoid stockouts. Fill rate can be calculated by dividing the number of items shipped by the number of items ordered within a specified time frame. A high fill rate ensures customer satisfaction, reduces lost sales, and maintains a competitive edge. By monitoring fill rate, organizations can identify any gaps in their inventory management processes, such as inadequate reorder quantities or supplier performance issues, and take proactive steps to improve availability and meet customer demands efficiently.

5. Supplier Performance: Supplier performance evaluation is an essential metric that assesses the performance of suppliers based on factors such as delivery reliability, quality of goods or services provided, and responsiveness to changes or issues. It assists organizations in selecting and managing their suppliers effectively. By closely monitoring supplier performance, organizations can identify reliable and consistent suppliers, improve supply chain collaboration, and mitigate potential risks. Organizations can develop a supplier performance scorecard to track and assess supplier performance regularly, fostering strong relationships with suppliers and optimizing the supply chain.

6. Lead Time: Lead time measures the time taken from placing an order to receiving the goods or services. It includes order processing, production, and transportation time. Monitoring lead time helps identify bottlenecks and inefficiencies in the supply chain. By reducing lead time, organizations can improve customer responsiveness, reduce inventory holding costs, and enhance overall supply chain agility. Analyzing lead time also helps optimize production schedules and improve the accuracy of demand forecasts. It allows organizations to proactively manage their supply chain operations, enhance customer satisfaction through shorter cycle times, and respond faster to changing market dynamics.

7. Cost of Goods Sold (COGS): The cost of goods sold (COGS) metric measures the direct costs associated with producing or procuring goods. It includes expenses such as raw materials, labor, and manufacturing overhead. Monitoring COGS helps assess the profitability and efficiency of supply chain operations. By analyzing COGS, organizations can identify cost-saving opportunities, optimize sourcing strategies, streamline production processes, and ensure competitive pricing. This helps organizations enhance their financial performance, allocate resources effectively, and gain an edge over competitors.

8. Return on Investment (ROI): ROI measures the return generated from investments made in the supply chain. It considers both the financial gains and costs incurred. A positive ROI indicates that supply chain investments are contributing to business growth and profitability.

Organizations can calculate ROI by comparing the financial benefits gained from a specific investment against the cost of that investment. Regular evaluation of ROI helps prioritize investments, assess their impact on the bottom line, and make informed investment decisions. By analyzing ROI across different supply chain initiatives, organizations can determine which investments are generating the highest returns and allocate resources accordingly.

9. Perfect Order Rate: The perfect order rate metric evaluates the percentage of orders that are delivered correctly, on time, and without any damage. It takes into account multiple aspects, including order accuracy, on-time delivery, and product condition, providing a comprehensive view of supply chain performance. A high perfect order rate signifies a well-functioning supply chain that consistently meets customer expectations. Measuring and improving this metric helps organizations enhance customer satisfaction, loyalty, and retention. Achieving a high perfect order rate requires organizations to analyze their end-to-end order fulfillment processes, identify any bottlenecks or areas for improvement, and implement corrective actions to deliver flawless orders consistently.

10. Supply Chain Cost: Supply chain cost is a fundamental metric that assesses the overall cost of managing and operating the supply chain. It includes expenses related to procurement, transportation, warehousing, and inventory holding. Monitoring supply chain costs helps organizations identify opportunities for cost savings and efficiency improvements. By analyzing supply chain costs, organizations can optimize their processes, negotiate better contracts with suppliers, streamline transportation routes, and implement effective inventory management practices. Effective management of supply chain costs allows organizations to enhance profitability, minimize waste, and gain a competitive advantage in the market.

It is crucial for organizations to select a set of performance metrics and KPIs that align with their specific goals and objectives. By focusing on these metrics and regularly reviewing and analyzing their performance, organizations can identify trends, make necessary adjustments, and continuously improve their supply chain operations. Leveraging performance metrics and KPIs enables organizations to optimize their supply chain, maximize customer satisfaction, and achieve sustainable growth.

————————

# 14. Case Studies in Effective Supply Chain Management

In this chapter, we delve deeper into real-life case studies that provide valuable insights into the importance and impact of effective supply chain management. These case studies highlight successful strategies and practices employed by companies to achieve competitive advantage, improve customer satisfaction, and drive business growth through their supply chains.

Case Study 1: Dell Inc.
Dell Inc. revolutionized the computer industry by adopting a direct-to-customer manufacturing and distribution model. This innovative approach allowed Dell to build a customer-centric supply chain that enabled them to reduce inventory costs and respond quickly to changing customer demands. By implementing a build-to-order strategy, Dell could customize products to individual customer specifications, eliminating the need for excessive inventory and ensuring customer satisfaction. This agile supply chain management approach played a pivotal role in establishing Dell's dominance in the personal computer market.

Dell's success can be attributed to its strong focus on supply chain planning and optimization. The company has invested heavily in advanced forecasting and demand planning systems to accurately predict customer demand and align their production accordingly. By closely collaborating with suppliers and sharing real-time information, Dell has created a responsive and flexible supply chain ecosystem. This has allowed them to minimize lead times, reduce stockouts, and optimize inventory levels.

Additionally, Dell's supply chain excellence extends beyond manufacturing and distribution. The company has also implemented efficient reverse logistics processes to handle product returns and refurbishment. By effectively managing the reverse flow of products, Dell can recover value from returned items and reduce waste.

Case Study 2: Zara
Zara, a global fashion retailer, has set itself apart through its agile supply chain management practices. By leveraging real-time data analysis and closely monitoring fashion trends, Zara can swiftly design, produce, and deliver new clothing collections within weeks. This fast-paced supply chain allows Zara to constantly refresh its product offerings,

attract customers with trendy fashion items, and maintain a high inventory turnover rate. Through effective supply chain management, Zara has been able to adapt quickly to market demands and gain a competitive edge in the fashion retail industry.

Central to Zara's success is its vertically integrated supply chain. Unlike traditional retailers, Zara controls every aspect of the supply chain, from design and manufacturing to distribution and retailing. This integration allows Zara to have maximum control and flexibility throughout the entire process. With in-house production capabilities, Zara can respond rapidly to market trends and customer preferences, minimizing lead times and reducing the risk of obsolete inventory.

Zara's supply chain also relies on strong partnerships with suppliers. The company works closely with a select group of suppliers that can quickly produce small batches of clothing to support Zara's fast-fashion approach. By maintaining long-term relationships and sharing information, Zara and its suppliers can collaborate effectively to meet the demands of the dynamic fashion industry.

Case Study 3: Amazon
Amazon's success in the e-commerce industry can be attributed to its efficient and customer-centric supply chain management practices. By employing advanced inventory management techniques and strategically located fulfillment centers, Amazon offers an extensive product selection, fast delivery times, and exceptional customer service. The company's focus on automation, advanced analytics, and continuous improvement has been instrumental in effectively managing their complex supply chains and meeting customer expectations. Amazon's relentless pursuit of supply chain excellence has allowed them to maintain a leading position in a highly competitive market.

A key aspect of Amazon's supply chain strategy is its robust distribution network. The company has strategically positioned fulfillment centers in close proximity to customers, enabling them to provide faster delivery and reduce transportation costs. Through effective location planning and optimization, Amazon has been able to meet the growing expectations for same-day and next-day deliveries. Moreover, Amazon's extensive use of automation technologies, including robotics, has further enhanced their operational efficiency and order accuracy.

In addition to its own logistics capabilities, Amazon has also built strong relationships with third-party logistics providers and carriers. This allows them to leverage additional capacity during peak seasons and efficiently handle fluctuating demand. The company's data-driven approach to supply chain management enables them to optimize inventory levels, improve forecasting accuracy, and personalize recommendations to customers, resulting in enhanced customer satisfaction and loyalty.

Case Study 4: Procter & Gamble (P&G)

Procter & Gamble (P&G) has achieved supply chain excellence through collaborative partnerships with suppliers and customers. P&G's supply chain management strategy involves leveraging technology and data sharing to streamline demand forecasting, minimize inventory levels, and improve delivery reliability. By implementing vendor-managed inventory systems and practicing collaborative planning, forecasting, and replenishment, P&G has achieved significant cost savings while simultaneously enhancing customer satisfaction. P&G's commitment to collaborative supply chain practices has elevated their competitiveness and positioned them as a leader in the consumer goods industry.

P&G's supply chain excellence is founded on strong collaborations and information sharing across the supply network. The company has implemented collaborative planning, forecasting, and replenishment (CPFR) processes with key suppliers, creating visibility and coordination throughout the supply chain. By sharing sales and inventory data in real-time, both P&G and its suppliers can work together proactively to adjust production and inventory levels to match demand accurately.

Another critical component of P&G's supply chain strategy is their focus on sustainability and responsible sourcing. The company has made significant strides in implementing environmentally friendly practices throughout their supply chain, such as reducing packaging waste, optimizing transportation routes to minimize carbon emissions, and partnering with suppliers that adhere to sustainable practices. P&G's commitment to sustainable supply chain management not only benefits the environment but also resonates with conscious consumers who prioritize environmentally friendly products.

Case Study 5: Toyota

Toyota has set the benchmark for supply chain management in the automotive industry with its lean principles and just-in-time manufacturing. By adopting a relentless focus on waste reduction, optimizing production processes, and establishing strong coordination and collaboration among suppliers, Toyota has achieved high levels of efficiency and quality in their operations. The Toyota Production System (TPS), built around the principles of continuous improvement and respect for people, has become a model for other companies seeking to improve their supply chain performance. Toyota's commitment to excellence in supply chain management has played a significant role in their sustained success and competitive advantage.

At the core of Toyota's supply chain management success is the Toyota Production System (TPS). TPS embraces the principles of lean manufacturing, which aim to eliminate waste, reduce inventory, and increase efficiency. By implementing a pull-based production system, Toyota can synchronize production with customer demand, reducing stock levels and minimizing the risk of overproduction. This lean approach reduces costs and ensures a smooth flow of materials, improving overall supply chain performance.

Moreover, Toyota has established strong collaborative relationships with its suppliers, creating a sense of partnership and collective responsibility for quality and efficiency. Through regular communication and shared goals, Toyota and its suppliers engage in continuous improvement efforts, minimizing defects and waste within the supply chain. By fostering a culture of shared responsibility and mutual respect, Toyota has built a resilient and efficient supply chain ecosystem.

In conclusion, these case studies offer valuable insights into how effective supply chain management can drive significant benefits for organizations across diverse industries. They highlight the importance of aligning supply chain strategy with overall business objectives, leveraging technology and data for better decision-making, engaging in collaborative partnerships, and continuously improving processes. By learning from these real-life success stories, businesses can gain valuable insights to optimize their supply chains and drive sustainable growth.

———————

# 15. Future Trends and Challenges in Supply Chain Management

The field of supply chain management is continuously evolving, and it is essential for professionals to be aware of the future trends and challenges that may impact their operations. In this chapter, we will explore some key areas of focus for the future.

1. Technological advancements: Technology has been a game-changer in supply chain management, and this trend is expected to continue in the future. Artificial intelligence (AI), machine learning (ML), and automation are revolutionizing various processes within the supply chain, including demand forecasting, inventory management, and transportation optimization.

AI and ML algorithms can analyze vast amounts of data, enabling supply chain professionals to make more accurate demand forecasts and optimize inventory levels. These technologies can also automate repetitive tasks, such as order placement and scheduling, freeing up time for supply chain managers to focus on strategic decision-making. Furthermore, the integration of robotics and drones in warehousing and transportation is enhancing efficiency, reducing errors, and improving last-mile delivery capabilities.

Advanced analytics and predictive modeling are becoming critical tools for decision-making, enabling supply chain professionals to anticipate demand, identify risks, and make more informed decisions in real-time. By leveraging these technologies, supply chain managers can optimize their operations, reduce costs, and improve customer satisfaction.

2. E-commerce and omni-channel distribution: The rise of e-commerce has completely transformed the retail landscape, and supply chains have had to adapt accordingly. In the future, we can expect to see further growth in online retail and the emergence of new distribution models such as omni-channel, which seamlessly integrates physical and online sales channels.

To meet the increasingly high customer expectations for fast and reliable deliveries, supply chain managers will need to develop strategies to handle the complexity of omni-channel operations. This includes implementing robust inventory management systems that provide real-time visibility across all channels, optimizing last-mile delivery capabilities by leveraging technologies like route optimization and crowdshipping, and adopting agile distribution networks that can quickly adapt to changing customer demands.

Moreover, supply chain managers will need to continuously enhance the customer experience by offering flexible delivery options, personalized recommendations, and easy returns. To achieve this, they must leverage data analytics to gain insights into customer buying patterns and preferences, allowing them to tailor their operations accordingly.

3. Sustainability and environmental concerns: With increasing awareness of climate change and environmental impact, supply chains will face growing pressure to adopt sustainable practices. Organizations and consumers are becoming more conscious of their carbon footprint, and they expect companies to demonstrate responsible environmental behaviors throughout the supply chain.

This requires a comprehensive approach to sustainability, starting with the selection of environmentally friendly suppliers and materials. Supply chain professionals will need to collaborate with suppliers to ensure environmental responsibility throughout the supply chain. This may involve conducting life cycle analyses to identify areas of improvement, implementing circular economy practices like recycling and remanufacturing, and fostering collaboration with suppliers to promote sustainable sourcing and procurement.

In addition, optimizing transportation and distribution networks to minimize carbon emissions will be crucial. Supply chain managers will need to explore alternative transportation modes and adopt fuel-efficient technologies. They may also consider consolidating shipments and implementing shared logistics networks to reduce the overall carbon footprint.

4. Globalization and geopolitical risks: The global economy continues to become increasingly connected, leading to greater reliance on international suppliers and extended supply chains. However, this globalization brings its own set of challenges. Supply chain managers must navigate geopolitical risks, such as trade wars, political instability, and changing regulations.

To mitigate these risks, supply chain professionals need to have contingency plans in place and build flexibility into their sourcing strategies. This involves diversifying suppliers and markets, creating redundant supply options and safety stock, and maintaining close relationships with key stakeholders. Additionally, supply chain managers should stay informed about geopolitical developments and proactively adapt their strategies to minimize disruptions.

Furthermore, geopolitical risks can also impact transportation routes, customs procedures, and warehousing practices. As a result, supply chain professionals must have a robust risk management framework in place. This includes conducting regular risk assessments, fostering collaboration with partners and government agencies, and continuously monitoring and reviewing strategies to adapt to changing circumstances.

5. Talent shortage and skills gap: As supply chains become more complex and technology-driven, there is a growing need for skilled professionals to manage and optimize these operations. However, the supply chain industry is currently facing a talent shortage and skills gap.

Organizations will need to invest in talent development to address this challenge. This includes providing training and development programs to enhance skill sets and knowledge, promoting cross-functional collaboration to foster an understanding of end-to-end supply chain operations, and implementing mentorship initiatives to transfer knowledge and expertise.

To attract and retain diverse skill sets, companies can also create attractive career paths, offer competitive compensation packages, and foster a culture of continuous learning and innovation. Additionally, partnerships with educational institutions and professional associations can help bridge the skills gap and cultivate the next generation of supply chain leaders. By embracing diversity, inclusivity, and lifelong learning, organizations can build a strong talent pipeline and stay ahead of the curve in an increasingly competitive landscape.

In conclusion, the future of supply chain management will be shaped by technological advancements, changing consumer habits, sustainability concerns, geopolitical risks, and the availability of skilled talent. By staying proactive and adaptive to these trends and challenges, supply chain professionals can position their organizations for success in the dynamic business landscape of the future.

Embracing technology, adopting sustainable practices, managing geopolitical risks, and investing in talent development will be essential for driving innovation, maintaining a competitive edge, and ensuring a resilient supply chain that meets the evolving needs of customers and stakeholders.